ICNC **MONOGRAPH** SERIES

The Impact of Nonviolent Resistance on the Peaceful Transformation of Civil War

Luke Abbs

ICNC PRESS

Table of Contents

Tables and Figures

Executive Summary

Does largescale and sustained nonviolent resistance increase the likelihood of negotiated resolution of civil war? Do nonviolent movements increase the durability of peace and democratization after a civil war has ended? If so, what characteristics and types of nonviolent movements can explain this effect? In recent years, a burgeoning literature has explored the strategic advantages of using nonviolent resistance to achieve positive political outcomes, such as change of political system and democratization. Yet, despite data from this manuscript showing that one-fifth of largescale nonviolent campaigns occurred during the course of a civil war, we know little about how nonviolent action affects the transformation of armed conflict.

Bringing together the previously isolated literatures on nonviolent resistance, peacebuilding and democratization, this monograph explores how nonviolent resistance can aid peacebuilding efforts that transform armed conflict. This monograph argues that the largescale nonviolent campaigns increase the likelihood of a negotiated settlement to civil war, by undermining governmental power in ways that open up political space and empower civil society, and by promoting constructive change which redefines societal relations. This constructive and inclusive legacy of nonviolent campaigns subsequently increases the likelihood of democratization once the civil war has ended. Using data on all civil war episodes from 1955 to 2013, this monograph finds clear evidence for these propositions, based on diverse evidence from large-N quantitative analyses and study comparisons.

1

1. Motivation for This Study

Nonviolent resistance, also referred to as civil resistance or strategic nonviolent conflict, involves a vast array of strategically planned nonviolent extra-institutional tactics. This can be categorized as forms of persuasion (e.g., protests, demonstrations), non-cooperation (e.g., strikes, boycotts), nonviolent intervention (e.g., sit-ins, the overloading of state institutions) (Sharp, 1973), as well as self-organizing and constructive resistance with alternative institution building to perceived injustice and violence (Dudouet 2019; Bartkowski 2018).

On 11 February 2011, Egypt's President Hosni Mubarak resigned from office after 29 years in power following mass anti-government protests. This was one of many nonviolent movements deploying tactics of nonviolent resistance that emerged across the Arab world that year, capturing international attention in what would later be known as the Arab Spring. During this period, long-standing dictators in Tunisia and Egypt were removed from power and governmental reforms were instituted. Some moved closer toward democratic systems (Tunisia) and some saw the re-emergence of dictatorship (Egypt) or experienced civil wars (Syria). Since 2011, many nonviolent uprisings—from Ukraine to Armenia, from Gambia to Burkina Faso, from Algeria to Sudan—have emerged and succeeded, often against formidable odds.

This apparent and extraordinary ability of nonviolent movements to foster political change has been echoed with timely research. A number of quantitative studies have shown that largescale anti-government nonviolent campaigns across the world have brought about political change, such as change of political systems and democratization (Chenoweth and Stephan 2011; Celestino and Gleditsch 2013), yet this transformation has not been explored within the context of armed conflict.

Five years prior to the Arab Spring, the pro-democracy April Uprising in Nepal (also called Jana Andolan II or People's Movement) successfully removed King Gyanendra and abolished the monarchy. Yet this case differs from other nonviolent campaigns in that it occurred within the context of civil war and subsequently paved the way for a renewed peace process which was signed seven months later in November 2006. Both signatories of the peace agreement had collaborated in the April Uprising against the monarchy: the Seven Party Alliance (formerly the country's opposition) and the Communist Party of Nepal (CPNM or Maoists) that had engaged in armed rebellion (Bogati and Thurber 2021).

Table 1. Definition of Nonviolent Campaigns

This monograph focuses on largescale and anti-government <u>**nonviolent campaigns**</u>,[1] which deploy nonviolent extra-institutional tactics to pursue a maximalist strategy to force major political change, including regime change, self-determination, and territorial secession. This differs from localized and everyday nonviolent resistance that may also be evident within ongoing civil wars but not part of a maximalist campaign. This monograph uses the terms nonviolent campaigns, civil resistance campaigns, largescale nonviolent movements, nonviolent resistance campaigns, and wartime nonviolent resistance interchangeably to denote largescale and maximalist nonviolent campaigns, unless stated otherwise in the text.

The process of conflict transformation refers to actions and processes that seek to address the long-term root causes of a civil war, in pursuit of peace by peaceful means (Dudouet 2017). Literature on peace processes also suggests that democratization is important for continued conflict transformation and durable peace once the armed conflict has ended, with democratic principles being central to many peace agreements, but especially when nonviolent actors have also been involved (Bell and O'Rourke 2007; Nilsson 2012). The case of Nepal is hailed as an example of how a wartime nonviolent campaign can contribute to the transformation of civil war, durable peace, and democratization once armed conflict has come to an end (Subedi and Bhattarai 2017; Francis 2002; Dudouet 2017).

Yet we know far less about the impact nonviolent campaigns may have during civil war and after a civil war has ended—whether nonviolent resistance influences peaceful transitions from armed conflict to peace, and whether, in the post-conflict phase, such transitions lead to durable peace and democratization. While existing research can explain why the Nepalese campaign was successful in removing the monarchy from power, achieving in 19 days what armed insurgency had failed to achieve in 10 years, this literature does not explain how nonviolent resistance revived the peace process that led to sustainable peace and multi-party politics in Nepal. The lack of scholarly attention leaves few answers as to whether Nepal is representative of other cases where nonviolent campaigns made a notable impact. Is there a systematic relationship between nonviolent campaigns and negotiated settlements to civil war? Do these campaigns subsequently lead to durable peace and post-conflict democratization?

---

1   Largescale campaigns involve at least 1,000 observed participants in a series of coordinated and continuous tactics (Chenoweth and Lewis 2013, 14). This excludes conventional, institutional, political activities, such as court litigations, lobbying, or petitions. Nonviolent resistance is not the same as principled nonviolence, pacifism, or a personal philosophy of nonviolence and is understood as a strategic, rather than moral, imperative.

Table 2. Definitions of Civil War, Conflict Termination, and Conflict Transformation

A <u>civil war</u> is an intra-state armed contestation between the government and armed rebels over issues related to political power (governmental dispute) or secession (territorial dispute) (following the Uppsala Conflict Data Program [UCDP] definition, see Petersson and Wallensteen 2015).[2] The UCDP uses a threshold of at least 25 yearly battle deaths to classify a conflict as a civil war. If the level of violence falls below 25 yearly deaths, **conflict termination** occurs and the conflict is no longer a civil war. This monograph is largely interested in terminations that are brought about by a **negotiated settlement** signed between the armed belligerents, and brought about by local, state-based or international peacebuilding strategies used to find a solution to violent conflicts.

Nonviolent resistance and peacebuilding that underpin negotiated settlements both belong to the broader field of **conflict transformation**, a "comprehensive term referring to actions and processes which seek to address the root causes of a particular conflict over the long term, in the pursuit of just peace by peaceful means...to transform negative, destructive conflict into positive, constructive conflict" (Dudouet 2017, 5).

This gap in our knowledge is a consequence of nonviolent resistance being explored largely in isolation to studies of civil war and peacebuilding. Nonviolent resistance has seldom featured in the peacebuilding academic literature. Practitioners often express concerns of further instability and violence that may arise after the emergence of nonviolent resistance within the already unstable context of civil war. Moreover, while research has recently focused on comparing violent and nonviolent movements, such studies have largely missed the co-occurrence of nonviolent mobilizations and civil wars. Despite this, available data shows largescale nonviolent campaigns have been present in one-fifth of all civil war episodes since 1955.[3]

The aim of this study is to shed more light on the relationship between nonviolent campaigns active during civil war (i.e., wartime nonviolent campaigns) and transformation of armed conflict toward peace agreements, durable peace, and post-conflict democratization. The monograph uses a new dataset on largescale wartime nonviolent movements, civil war, and the post-conflict period to answer a number of key questions:

---

2   This data therefore excludes low-scale violence and armed violence that does not involve the state.

3   Based on data used in this manuscript; nonviolent campaigns within the Major Episodes of Contention Dataset (MEC) and civil war episodes from the Uppsala Conflict Data Program (UCDP) Armed Conflict Dataset.

- Does the presence of nonviolent campaigns during civil war aid conflict transformation and an end to the armed conflict?

- Do wartime nonviolent movements have important legacies for more durable peace and democratization after civil war has come to an end?

- Do these relationships occur in contexts other than the well-known case of Nepal?

To unpack these questions, this monograph relies mainly on statistical evidence based on a global sample of cases between 1955 and 2013, and is supplemented with predictive analyses[4] and case study evidence from South Africa and Mali.[5] Information collected from the data and cases provide consistent evidence that nonviolent movements active during armed conflict are associated with a greater likelihood of a negotiated settlement to civil war and post-conflict democratization (Assumptions 1–2 and 4–5 in Table 4). No evidence is found that wartime nonviolent movements reduce the likelihood of conflict recurrence in the future (Assumption 3 in Table 4). The root causes of civil war are extremely difficult to resolve, and it is equally difficult for states to escape reoccurring violent conflict even when international actors and nonviolent actors play an active role in peace processes. As such, states emerging from civil war often lack the resources to build stable institutions that can prevent future violence.

---

4   Predictive analyses tell us the magnitude of the effect, by comparing the predicted probability of the outcome for cases where nonviolent campaigns are present with cases where they are not.

5   These cases were chosen because despite being very different cases, the outcome in both countries was positive, as was the case in Nepal.

Table 4. Relationships Between Nonviolent Campaigns and Civil War Explored in This Study

STAGE 1: ONGOING CIVIL WAR	METHODS USED
Assumption 1: Impact of wartime nonviolent campaigns and negotiated settlements on ending civil war	**Statistical and predictive analysis; case studies**
Assumption 2: Impact of the campaign's attributes (e.g., social diversity, decentralized campaign structure) on ending civil war	
STAGE 2: POST-CONFLICT[6]	METHODS USED
Assumption 3: Impact of wartime nonviolent campaigns on the post-conflict recurrence of civil war	**Statistical and predictive analysis**
Assumption 4: Impact of wartime nonviolent campaigns on post-conflict democratization	**Statistical and predictive analysis; case studies**
Assumption 5: Impact of campaign's attributes (e.g., social and organizational diversity, a decentralized leadership structure) on post-conflict democratization	

This monograph continues as follows. First, plausible assumptions that build on existing understandings and literature concerning the relationship between largescale nonviolent campaigns, the resolution of armed conflict and end to civil war, and the durability of post-conflict peace are presented. Next, the results supporting these assumptions listed in Table 4 are discussed in detail. The monograph concludes with a discussion on the implications of these findings for activists, practitioners and academics. Supplementary details on the statistical analyses and full results are reported in Appendix I and II.

In the next chapter, existing literature and assumptions derived from that literature will be explored, informing propositions (or hypotheses) that are later tested in the statistical analyses and case studies.

---

6   As stated in Tables 1 and 2, this is the period of peace following the end of the civil war episode.

2. Literature and Theory: Nonviolent Resistance and the Transformation of Civil War

Very little research exists on the impact that nonviolent resistance has on the transformation of armed conflict. This is largely due to misconceptions about the power of civilians (or a lack thereof) during the course of armed conflict. The common perception is that in the war context unarmed civilians are withdrawn (for protection and survival) and thus passive (in contrast to active armed rebel groups). The broader study of armed conflict often sees little role for civilians as agents of change, instead viewing civilians as either a resource or victims with little option but to either flee, support, or join one of the armed groups to survive (Hallward, Masullo, and Mouly 2017), helping to explain why the relationship between nonviolent resistance, civil war and durable peace is relatively under-researched.

While in some instances nonviolent resistance has been vulnerable to extreme violence—such as Tiananmen Square and Burma's 8888 uprising in the late 1980s—in many other cases nonviolent resistance has not only been able to emerge but, in fact, has helped to reduce or prevent mass killings (Perkoski and Chenoweth 2018) and has even managed to achieve its major political goals despite the challenges of operating in armed contexts (Vüllers and Krtsch 2020). Recent and emerging research on localized nonviolent resistance during civil war has also challenged this perception, outlining incredible localized attempts of civilians to influence the behavior of armed groups.[7] In other words, civilians are far from passive. Yet while this research shows that nonviolent resistance is both prevalent and can influence and even mitigate violence during civil war, this tells us little about the broader implications of anti-government nonviolent resistance on the transformation of civil war, durable peace and post-conflict democratization.

Another issue is that the broad and diverse peacebuilding literature has grown in almost complete isolation to studies on the practice of nonviolent resistance. Peacebuilding research has instead explored activities of civil society largely through institutional channels or channeled through non-governmental organizations, rather than grassroots movements engaged

---

7   This research has focused almost exclusively on localized nonviolent activism; outlining incredible attempts to influence the trajectory of ongoing civil war. This includes localized nonviolent resistance against the government and armed groups (see Vüllers and Krtsch 2020) that has led to the creation of "zones of peace" that has decreased civilian targeting, homicides and extra-judicial killings (Barter 2014, 2015; Mouly, Idler, and Garrido 2015; Mouly, Garrido, and Idler 2018; Masullo 2015; Arjona 2015; Kaplin 2013a, 2013b, 2017; Hancock and Mitchell 2007; Koefoed 2017) and the creation of civilian-led peacekeeping (UCP), which contribute to local community peace infrastructures and monitor human rights and ceasefire violations (Funari, Oldenhuis, and Julian 2015; Julian and Schweitzer 2015).

in nonviolent resistance (Dudouet 2017). Peacebuilding scholars and practitioners often express concerns about the viability and vulnerability of nonviolent resistance within the context of armed conflict. Nonviolent resistance is often considered too weak and its participants too vulnerable within the context of armed conflict (Francis 2009).

A small but emerging scholarship has suggested that nonviolent campaigns can have broader and positive impacts on the transformation of civil war. This builds upon literature on conflict transformation that points to the importance of nonviolent campaigns in supporting peacebuilding efforts (Lederach 1995; Frances 2002; Dudouet 2005). Literature on peace processes suggests that nonviolent actors can have important legacies for post-conflict peace and democratization (Bell and O'Rourke 2007; Nilsson 2012). However, evidence on the impact of anti-government nonviolent campaigns remains largely anecdotal or confined to the study of a few well-known and "successful" cases such as Nepal (Dudouet 2017; Subedi and Bhattarai 2017; Bogati and Thurber 2021; see also Hallward et al. 2017).

Dudouet (2019) highlights the key contributions of peace movements—a very diverse type of civil society organization—which often deploy a varied set of nonviolent functions from protests, boycotts, and other activities that resemble anti-government nonviolent movements to political engagement and consultation in national-level negotiations (Dudouet 2019). Yet the impact of these nonviolent tactics used in peace processes remains poorly understood beyond a few key case studies such as Liberia (Galvanek and Shilue 2021).

Suggestive evidence about the positive impact of nonviolent organizing on ending civil wars also derives from a recent large-N study by Leventoğlu and Metternich (2018), who find that greater protest activity is associated with a greater likelihood of peace negotiations and settlements in Africa. However, this explores general nonviolent protest over a range of issues that are often not related to maximalist goals focused on bringing about major systemic change.

Despite the emergence of positive findings, existing evidence largely derives from a small but growing case literature that has yet to be tested across a broad set of cases. It is important to note that it is extremely challenging to bridge conflict divides, win over opponents, and resolve social divisions after violence has been experienced (Dudouet 2007). Policymakers often express concerns that bringing many people together amid armed conflict may be dangerous, as the weakening of the government's pillars of power may lead to a power vacuum which could be filled by extremist factions and lead to further escalation in violence. Despite these concerns, this monograph provides various forms of evidence showing that anti-government nonviolent campaigns are important agents of change in the context of civil war and have an important legacy after war comes to an end. The next section explores anecdotal evidence, emerging case literature, and the key assumptions that underpin these relationships.

3. Assumptions About Nonviolent Campaigns and the Transformation of Civil War

While peacebuilding literature largely remains skeptical about the importance of nonviolent movements, seminal nonviolent resistance scholarship has noted the extraordinary ability of anti-government and largescale nonviolent campaigns to initiate major political change.

Unlike armed groups, nonviolent movements have fewer moral and physical barriers to participation and therefore are uniquely placed to generate leverage through mobilizing large numbers of people against the government, thus attracting diverse groups of people from different socio-economic backgrounds, occupations, genders, and ages, and thereby increasing the probability of gaining sympathy or support from pro-government segments of society (Chenoweth and Stephan 2011; Nepstad 2011).

Because of this strategic advantage, even in the most violent contexts, nonviolent movements have been very effective in bringing about wholesome political change. In the same year that movements were mobilizing during the Arab Spring, strong empirical evidence was provided in a seminal large-N study by Chenoweth and Stephan (2011) showing that nonviolent campaigns are twice as likely to bring about regime change than armed movements.

This section explores the assumptions that underpin arguments that nonviolent campaigns can support peacebuilding efforts and processes of conflict transformation in ways that increase the likelihood of negotiated agreements and provide important legacies for the post-conflict era, aiding prospects for more durable post-conflict peace and post-conflict democratization.

3.1. Impact of Nonviolent Campaigns on Negotiated Agreements Ending Civil Wars

Anecdotal evidence from highlighted cases such as Nepal and existing studies on conflict transformation demonstrate two assumptions about how nonviolent campaigns can influence civil war resolution. *First, nonviolent movements open up political space and transform "destructive conflict" into "constructive conflict" by mobilizing various social groups and using nonviolent methods against the state.*

This assumption derives from scholars and practitioners engaged in conflict transformation. While peacebuilding work has largely neglected the role of nonviolent movements in fostering peace, the conflict transformation approach has long regarded nonviolent resistance ("revolutionary approach") and peacebuilding ("resolutionary approach") as complementary strategies to conflict transformation (Lederach 1995; Francis 2002; Kriesberg 2003; Schirch 2004; Dudouet 2005; Kriesberg and Dayton 2012).

A series of International Center on Nonviolent Conflict (ICNC) special reports have suggested that the practice of nonviolent resistance and peacebuilding have worked in parallel and that both strategies have played an important role in addressing ongoing armed violent conflict (Dudouet 2017; Bogati and Thurber 2021; Galvanek and Shilue 2021). A United States Institute of Peace (USIP) training manual, *Synergizing Nonviolent Action and Peacebuilding (SNAP)*, has provided a strategic framework for nonviolent activists and peacebuilders to collectively transform violent conflict (Bloch and Schirch 2019).

The conflict transformation approach argues that wartime nonviolent campaigns can open up opportunities for peace and dialogue by seeking to transform destructive conflict (i.e., war and a polarized society) into constructive conflict (i.e., using peaceful means to address needs and grievances that underpin the broader political conflict). Wartime nonviolent movements often use nonviolent actions—increasing political engagement and setting up alternative grassroots institutions—to find inclusive solutions that reduce polarization and pave the way for intergroup cooperation (Francis 2009; Dudouet 2017).

Nonviolent movements explicitly attempt to unite opposition and participants from across conflict boundaries, empowering civil society by drawing on the strength of mass and diverse participation (Francis 2009). Attracting participants across conflict boundaries reduces the social distance between opponents and the state's pillars of power (i.e., pro-government supporters, security forces, religious leaders, and political and business elites), which if removed, undermines the government's legitimacy and ability to rule (see also DeNardo 1985; Schock 2005). South Africa's Second Defiance Campaign (1983–1994) specifically aimed to undermine apartheid through non-cooperation, including boycotts and multiracial peace marches that weakened the apartheid economy and that were eventually supported by white business and political elites formerly loyal to the government (Smuts and Westcott 1991).

The second assumption that derives from existing literature is that nonviolent campaigns can influence the resolution of civil war and dynamics of armed struggle because of their potential to undermine the relative power of the government that wages violent conflict.

In most civil wars, the government has greater power than oppositional challengers due to its access to state resources and the legitimacy it has on the international stage as a sovereign ruler. In contrast, rebel groups often have relatively less power due to fewer fighting resources and lack legitimacy due to their use of violence against the state. By weakening the government and forcing concessions, wartime nonviolent movements have been able to alter the power asymmetry that exists in most civil wars in a manner that opens up opportunities for dialogue that might not otherwise be possible (Dudouet 2011, 2013; Subedi and Bhattarai 2017).

In some cases, nonviolent campaigns have opened up political space by removing an incumbent from power, paving the way for peace talks. In Nepal, the monarchy had few incentives to seek peace, because it had consolidated its power and largely contained ongoing armed violence to remote rural areas. By forcing the monarchy to step down, the April Uprising removed a critical barrier to peace (Subedi and Bhattarai 2017). In other cases, nonviolent movements have forced the hand of the government to enter or maintain peace talks when they would otherwise have few incentives to do so (Francis 2002; Dudouet 2011; Dudouet 2013). For instance, in South Africa the Second Defiance Campaign's undermining of the economy forced the apartheid government—which had a strong security architecture— into talks with the opposition.

In some cases, nonviolent campaigns have opened up political space by removing an incumbent from power, paving the way for peace talks.

Nationwide nonviolent campaigns are also fairly successful in attracting international support, leading to a boomerang effect, whereby international support amplifies the demands of civil society and pressures warring parties to seek peace (Keck and Sikkink 1998; see also Schock 2005). For instance, the First Palestinian Intifada (1987–1993) drew significant moral support from the international community, transferring power from the Israeli government to Palestinian civil society actors that were using nonviolent tactics to push for peace and end Israeli occupation (Dudouet 2005; Dudouet 2011; Pearlman 2011). This increased the cost of violence and political pressure on the Israeli government and the Palestinian Liberation Organization to engage in the Oslo peace process, which led to an agreement in 1993.

On one hand, altering power asymmetries through domestic and international pressure can bring the government to the table. On the other hand, removing or weakening the government provides a more favorable and secure context for rebels to agree to talks, bargain, and eventually commit to an agreement, as they are more likely to gain favorable peace dividends and avoid security dilemmas which prevent them from credibly committing to a peace process. In other words, the rebels have less fears they could be annihilated after they put down their arms (Walter 2002).

Nonviolent campaigns have also helped civil society gain a seat at the negotiating table in various armed conflicts, providing civil society with more influence over the peace process and future design of post-settlement institutions. Research has shown the positive impact that nonviolent movements have had in national dialogues—for instance, in Yemen, Colombia, and Tunisia—directly influencing the decision-making processes and agenda in ongoing negotiations (Stigant and Murray 2015; Bloch and Schirch 2019). Both assumptions from existing literature motivate the first proposition of this monograph, with the aim of exploring the relationship between civil resistance and ending violent conflict across all instances of civil war from 1955 to 2013:

Proposition 1a: The existence of nonviolent resistance during civil war *increases the likelihood that civil war ends through a negotiated settlement.*

Anecdotal evidence and findings from existing studies suggest the assumption that wartime nonviolent campaigns are likely to have important legacies for the post-conflict phase once armed violence has come to an end—particularly on post-conflict democratization and the likelihood of the civil war relapsing. Both are explored in the following section.

3.2. Impact of Nonviolent Campaigns on the Post-Conflict Phase

Impact of Nonviolent Campaigns on Reducing the Chances for Recurrence of Armed Conflict

We know from existing research on nonviolent resistance that political transitions brought about by nonviolent movements appear to reduce the likelihood of armed conflict. Chenoweth and Stephan (2011) found that 28 percent of countries experienced civil war within ten years of a nonviolent political transition compared to 42 percent in countries that violently transitioned. Similarly, Johnstad (2010) found 95.7 percent of countries experiencing a nonviolent transition were subsequently free from civil war (Yet this analysis also includes countries that have not recently experienced civil war).

Countries with a recent history of civil war are much more prone to civil war compared to countries with no recent experience of armed conflict, and therefore represent a harder test that this monograph explores. There is extensive literature on conflict recurrence, with large-N studies focusing on factors concerning: conflict and country characteristics, such as more deadly conflicts, weaker institutions, and lack of economic growth; when countries get caught in conflict traps (Walter 2004; Quinn, Mason, and Gurses 2007; Collier, Hoeffler and Söderbom 2008); and the role of third parties in deterring violence, such as UN peacekeepers (Walter 2002; Doyle and Sambanis 2006; Fotna 2008). Gates et al. (2016) find that 60 percent of all civil wars, reoccur on average within seven years, but that peace agreements lay the groundwork for stable peace and that political reforms are necessary to achieve lasting peace.[8] Research has yet to determine whether wartime nonviolent movements may bring about more peaceful political environments that reduce the likelihood of conflict recurrence.

While civil war recurrence is a highly complex process, Nilsson (2012) finds that where civil society actors have been involved in the peace process, the risk of peace failing was reduced by 64 percent. Moreover, nonviolent campaigns have been associated with processes that reduce the likelihood of conflict recurrence in the post-conflict period. Johnstad (2010) finds that nonviolent campaign-led transitions foster greater economic growth in the countries where they occur. Another important consequence of nonviolent campaigns is that they increase the likelihood of democratization (Pinckney 2021) and post-conflict democratization as organizations within the nonviolent movement are able to credibly threaten re-mobilization during a transition as a response to potential or real democratic backsliding (Butcher, Grey, and Mitchell 2018). From the literature on armed conflict, we know that democratic states are less likely to experience war (Hegre et al. 2001). This motivates the following proposition:

Proposition 1b: The existence of nonviolent resistance during civil war *decreases the chance of civil reoccurrence in the post-conflict period*.

Impact of Nonviolent Campaigns on the Likelihood of Post-Conflict Democratization

There is an extensive and well-established literature on democratization. However, this litera jture has mainly focused on top-down dynamics, highlighting structural economic and social factors (see Vanhanen 1990) and elite pacts (O'Donnell and Schmitter 1986; Przeworski 1991) as prerequisites for democratic transitions. Until recently, little research has explored the bottom-up impact of nonviolent movements on democratization.[9]

While this monograph is specifically interested in whether nonviolent campaigns are related to post-conflict democratization, civil resistance research has recently demonstrated that nonviolent campaigns generally lead to more democratic outcomes. Chenoweth and Stephan (2011) found that countries are ten times more likely to achieve democratization within five years after a successful nonviolent campaign than in the case of transitions brought

---

8   Other studies have explored the institutional design of peace settlements and its impact on recurrence (Hartzell and Hoddie 2003), while others suggest that peace is more durable when the previous conflict ends in victory rather than in negotiated settlement (Quinn, Mason, and Gurses 2007; Kreutz 2010).

9   Some prominent exceptions include Ulfelder (2005) who finds nonviolent protest events increase the likelihood of democratization in dictatorships, and Teorell (2010) concludes that anti-government protests increase levels of democracy in the short- and long-term.

about by armed conflict—further, countries achieve multiparty elections in 57 percent of all nonviolent campaign-led transitions.[10]

Bayer, Bethke and Lambach (2016) also found that nonviolent campaigns increase the durability and duration of democracies after transition has been achieved, while nonviolent resistance-led democratic transitions survived on average 47 years, democracies after victory in an armed conflict lasted only five years in countries with elite-led transitions, and nine years in countries with neither violent or nonviolent campaigns.[11] Bethke and Pinckney (forthcoming) find that this is because nonviolent resistance-led transitions increase the quality of democracy, particularly in terms of freedom of expression.

Despite these findings, it remains unclear if this impact is consistent in more challenging post-conflict environments where countries have a distinct history of violence, as this relationship has received almost no scholarly attention. However, there is some anecdotal evidence and suggestive findings from civil resistance and conflict transformation literature which indicate wartime nonviolent movements may have an important legacy for democratization after a civil war ends.

For instance, central to mobilizing mass and diverse numbers of participants in nonviolent campaigns is coalition building. In practice, coalition building during civil war means an attempt to build bridges and reconciliation, reduce social distance and polarization, offer reassurances to opponents, and redefine violent relationships into cooperative and constructive ones (Lederach 1997; Dudouet 2011; Dudouet 2017; Bloch and Schirch 2019). The constructive dimension of nonviolent movements means they are likely to bring about participatory practices that are conducive to participatory democracy and peacebuilding activities in post-conflict settings (Francis 2002; see also Dudouet 2017).

Coalition agreements often become formalized and act as a template for power-sharing mechanisms and democratization (Subedi and Bhattarai 2017). For example, the 12-point agreement between the seven-party opposition alliance and Maoist rebels—which underpinned a broad anti-monarchy coalition in the April Uprising in Nepal—eventually served as a blueprint for future multi-party political system in the country. Nonviolent movements also give civil society a voice, which can be used as a vehicle to influence a peace process and

---

10   Karatnycky and Ackerman (2005) find that transitions brought about by nonviolent campaigns were four times more likely to score highly on Freedom House's measure of political rights and civil liberties, than armed resistance-led transitions. Celestino and Gledtisch (2013) later confirmed these findings, showing nonviolent campaign-led transitions created more favorable democratic outcomes than transitions not brought about by dissent.

11   Based on a survival statistical analysis, which in this instance explores the length of time a democracy survives, they compared democratic transitions brought about by nonviolent movements with transitions deriving from armed conflict and no campaigns at all (elite-led).

the future design of post-settlement institutions and participatory practices (Nilsson 2012; Randle 1994; Schock 2005; Celestino and Gleditsch 2013).

Yet, some movements have successfully pressured for peace negotiations but have then failed to nudge elites into delivering peace dividends once negotiations ended (Clark 2005; Subedi and Bhattarai 2017). For instance, in Sierra Leone, while activists were successful in influencing the peace process, they were less successful in influencing the implementation of the agreement and post-conflict democratization. Many of the movement's leaders were co-opted by offers of new government positions. Nevertheless, the evidence explored above leads to the following proposition:

> **Proposition 1c:** The existence of nonviolent resistance during civil war *increases the likelihood of post-conflict democratization.*

3.3. Campaign Attributes, Negotiated Settlements, and the Post-Conflict Legacy of Campaigns

Specific features of a campaign may have a greater impact on political change than other features in the context of armed conflict and the post-conflict period. One of the main assumptions derived from the literature on conflict transformation discussed above, is that wartime nonviolent movements can influence peace by undermining governmental power, thereby altering power asymmetries between the more powerful government and the less powerful opposition. Therefore, it is logical that when a nonviolent campaign is successful in achieving its maximalist goals—by bringing about regime change or forcing government concessions, thus providing more security guarantees to the rebels—peace should be more likely.

> **Proposition 2:** Nonviolent campaigns during civil wars *that successfully achieve their political aims* increase the likelihood of reaching a negotiated agreement to end the war (P2a), establishing durable peace after the violent conflict (reducing the likelihood of civil war recurrence) (P2b), and facilitating post-conflict democratization (P2c).

Nonviolent campaigns are more likely to be successful when they attract large and diverse segments of the population (Chenoweth and Stephan 2011). This may also be the case in the context of civil war. Even wartime regimes are reliant on the compliance of its citizens in order to rule and carry out their day-to-day policies, including their waging of armed conflict. A larger number of participants and greater levels of non-cooperation provide leverage against the government. Nonviolent campaigns have on average eleven times more participants than violent campaigns, which is why few regimes are able to withstand the demands of large nonviolent movements in contrast to violent rebellions.[12]

Proposition 3: Nonviolent campaigns during civil wars with a *greater number of participants*, increase the likelihood of reaching a negotiated agreement to end the war (P3a), establishing durable peace after the violent conflict (P3b), and facilitating post-conflict democratization (P3c).

Nonviolent movements are also uniquely placed to mobilize diverse participants from various social groups and organizations and can encourage loyalty switches within broad segments of the population. Social and organizational diversity provides tactical innovation and more leverage in that they can draw on different social and ethnic groups and different socioeconomic backgrounds, occupations, ages, and political ideologies, who—when withholding support—can hurt the government in different ways (Butcher and Svensson 2016; Abbs 2020).

Diverse movements can generate sympathy and win broad participation that mitigate polarization and reduce social distance across conflict lines. This is likely to increase the loyalty shifts across conflict divides in favor of the movement, allowing pressure to be applied before, during, and after peace negotiations (Hallward et al. 2017; Dudouet 2017; Subedi and Bhattarai 2017). Pinckney (2018) finds that subsequent democratization depends on a nonviolent movement's ability to maintain its mobilization of its core social bases in order to continue exercising constructive pressure on elites for positive and lasting change.

Proposition 4: Nonviolent campaigns during civil wars that are *more socially diverse* increase the likelihood of reaching a negotiated agreement to end the war (P4a), establishing durable peace after the violent conflict (P4b), and facilitating post-conflict democratization (P4c).

Lessons can also be learned from the impact of women's participation in campaigns. Emerging research highlights the positive effects women's participation can have on nonviolent campaigns and the outcomes produced by these campaigns. Women's participation in campaigns tends to increase nonviolent discipline and the likelihood of loyalty shifts within pro-government segments of the population (Codur and King 2015; Principe 2017), meaning women's participation increases the likelihood of campaign success (Chenoweth 2019). Moreover, the participation of women's groups can increase long-term women's empowerment that has led to substantive progress in gender equity and women's political

---

12   Erica Chenoweth finds that where campaigns were able to mobilize and meet a 3.5 percent participation threshold, in terms of the percentage of the population, target governments have rarely been able to avoid political change (see Robson 2019).

representation, leading to more inclusive societies, which appears more conducive for democratization than armed conflict (McAllister 1999; Paxton, Hughes, and Green 2006; Chenoweth 2019).

There are numerous examples where women's groups have managed to mobilize across conflict lines, have forced negotiations, and have pressured belligerents through the implementation of a peace agreement. For instance, the WLMAP in Liberia has been credited with pressuring the parties to the peace process at all stages in their Campaign for Peace (Galvanek and Shilue 2021). They successfully utilized their leverage by mobilizing women from Muslim and Christian organizations and across ethnicities, including the ruling Americo-Liberian class.

Proposition 5: *The participation of women in nonviolent campaigns during civil war*, increases the likelihood of reaching a negotiated agreement to end the war (P5a), establishing durable peace after the violent conflict (P5b), and facilitating post-conflict democratization (P5c).

Organizational diversity can also be critical for bringing about subsequent and durable democratization. Existing literature on social movements and civil resistance suggest that organizational diversity is important for maintaining desired outcomes and achieving post-conflict democratization (see Olzak and Ryo 2007; Butcher, Grey, and Mitchell 2018). Yet, more recent research finds little evidence that organizational diversity alone improves democratization due to the "diversity dilemma"—where organizational diversity increases democratic preferences but undermines capacity through infighting. Instead, they point to the importance of trade unions and religious organizations that can achieve diverse participation while maintaining unity (Pinckney, Butcher, and Braithwaite 2019).

Proposition 6: Wartime nonviolent campaigns with a *higher number of participating organizations*, increase the likelihood of reaching a negotiated agreement to end the war (P6a), establishing durable peace after the violent conflict (P6b), and facilitating post-conflict democratization (P6c).

Another important feature of most nonviolent campaigns is the establishment of alternative institutions as part of their constructive resistance programs. Such alternative institutions and the constructive processes that bring them about may also be important in fostering peaceful change. Constructive programs are self-sufficient and grassroots-based activities, involving the creation of parallel and inclusive institutions that challenge and circumvent unjust and oppressive socio-economic and political state systems—for instance, the development of an alternative education system as seen in Kosovo and the "committees" that were set up in South African townships as an alternative to the harsh and unjust apartheid political structure.

Because alternative institutions are inclusive and socially diverse, they often lay the groundwork for future participatory democracy (Bartkowski 2018; Francis 2002; Dudouet 2011). They also aim to address root causes of conflict and enable civil society groups to become key actors in their own right in the development processes which can increase the durability of peace (Koefoed 2017).

Constructive programs can also provide an institutional template for a durable peace (Dudouet 2011) and the successful democratic transition after violent conflict. For instance, in South Africa, clinics for the community providing health provisions, local justice mechanisms, and legal advice, which increasingly replaced discriminatory apartheid institutions. These helped provide a basis for new inclusive institutions that replaced the old and segregated institutions after the National Peace Accord was signed. From this assumption raises another proposition:

> **Proposition 7:** Nonviolent campaigns during civil war that *create alternative institutions* as part of their resistance strategies increase the likelihood of reaching a negotiated agreement to end the war (P7a), establishing durable peace after the violent conflict (P7b), and facilitating post-conflict democratization (P7c).

Finally, research on nonviolent resistance offers some suggestive findings regarding the leadership structure of nonviolent campaigns. Nonviolent campaigns deploy many methods to mitigate violence from the regime (repression) and violence within the campaign itself (violent flanks). There is consensus within the field of nonviolent resistance that nonviolent discipline is essential in achieving the stated goals of a nonviolent movement (Popovic et al. 2007, Ackerman and DuVall 2000, Nepstad 2011; Pinckney 2018; Abbs and Gleditsch 2019), even within the context of state repression or armed violence. Central to nonviolent discipline is how adaptable campaigns are to ongoing violence, which Pearlman (2011) suggests is dependent on the type of leadership present in a movement.

In a study on Palestinian movements, Pearlman suggests that non-existent hierarchical leadership makes nonviolent campaigns more susceptible to a lack of nonviolent discipline. Without centralized leadership, campaigns may be internally divided and less able to monitor or counter a lack of discipline. Moreover, Schock (2005) argues that centralized leadership is important in the long term, in maintaining a strong front and articulating clear demands after initial goals have been achieved. In many cases, disunited movements lacking central leadership have not been able to push through democratization after initial political change or for that matter, a peace agreement, has been achieved.

Contrary to these earlier findings, in his large-N study of nonviolent campaigns Pinckney (2018) finds that campaigns with hierarchical leadership had in fact lower nonviolent discipline. In contrast, decentralized leadership structures are more adaptable and flexible to violent

19

challenges that nonviolent resistance might face, particularly because the leadership is more difficult to target with repression. This assumption informs the final proposition:

Proposition 8: Nonviolent campaigns during civil war with *decentralized leadership structures* increase the likelihood of reaching a negotiated agreement to end the war (P8a), establishing durable peace after the violent conflict (P8b), and facilitating post-conflict democratization (P8c).

4. Mapping the Analysis

This monograph identifies a total of 1,798 conflict years from 346 civil war episodes, across 99 countries that occurred between 1955 and 2013. In many countries civil war reoccurs, and thus a single country may experience several episodes of civil war. Some countries have multiple ongoing civil wars. For example, in Sudan, the civil war in Darfur overlaps with the civil war between north and south Sudanese groups. The conflict years of these episodes represent the unit of analysis; the observations constitute the basis for the statistical analysis.

This conflict data covers the two stages of a civil war that is explored here:

1. active and ongoing armed conflict

2. the period of peace that follows the end of civil war (post-conflict phase)

The *first stage* of the statistical analysis explores the impact of nonviolent campaigns during civil war—whether the existence of nonviolent campaigns increases the likelihood of a politically negotiated agreement between warring parties to end the war.

The *second stage* explores how nonviolent campaigns during civil war influence the post-civil war period, referred to throughout this study as the post-conflict phase. The second stage explores two outcomes: the recurrence of civil war (after a previous civil war episode has terminated) and whether a democratic transition occurs in the post-conflict phase (both at any point during this phase and within five years of the end of the civil war).

This study also looks at the campaign features and whether specific features impact negotiated settlements and post-conflict peace and democratization. These results are visualized using predictions from the statistical analyses, which compare the predicted probability of the outcome for cases where nonviolent campaigns are present with cases where nonviolent campaigns are not.

In Appendix II, additional out-of-sample predictive analyses are explored with a detailed discussion of how the predictive and statistical methods work. Four segments of the data (80 percent of all data) are used to predict another segment of this data (the remaining 20 percent of the data, using k-fold cross-validation—explained in detail in Appendix I). The purpose of this is to provide additional empirical support to findings from the statistical analysis.

4.1. Stage 1: Measuring Civil War Episodes and Negotiated Settlements

To measure civil war, this study relies on conflict episodes coded in the Uppsala Conflict Data Program's (UCDP) Armed Conflict Dataset (Gleditsch et al. 2002; see also Petersson and Wallensteen 2015). A conflict episode is considered active in years where violence between government forces and at least one non-state armed actor (i.e., a rebel group) reaches a minimum 25 battle-related deaths in one calendar year. Civil war involves political contestations over the government (i.e., rebels seeking to overthrow the government) or territory (i.e., independence or regional autonomy). Civil war episodes account for breaks in conflict where violence terminates and then may reoccur in later years.

In Stage 1 of the statistical analysis, the dependent variable (the outcome that is of interest to this study) is whether or not a civil war episode ends through a *politically negotiated settlement*. Here data is taken from the UCDP Termination dataset (Kreutz, 2010), which collates information on type of civil war terminations, negotiated agreements (i.e., ceasefires and peace agreements), government military victory, rebel victory, and instances of low activity (falls below 25 annual deaths).

A civil war episode is effectively ended when armed violence falls below the UCDP threshold of 25 annual battlefield deaths. Out of the 357 civil war episodes between 1955 and 2013 considered for this study, 85 civil war terminations (around a quarter) are being attributed to a negotiated settlement. This is a dummy measure (consisting of a value of 1 or 0), where 1 is coded for years when a negotiated agreement is signed and 0 for years with no agreement.

A slight limitation to this data, but which in fact strengthens the reliability of the findings, is that it only includes negotiated agreements that are signed either during active conflict or in the first year after violence is ended. This excludes some cases where negotiated agreements are signed more than a year after the cessation of armed violence, which are therefore not included in the statistical analysis (e.g., Nicaragua 1978, Bangladesh 1990, Palestine 1991, Haiti 1991, Sierra Leone 1996, Papua New Guinea 1997, Aceh 1999).

However, this limitation actually strengthens the reliability of the findings because if these additional cases were added, they would actually lend further support to arguments about the positive impact that nonviolent campaigns have on negotiated agreements. In other words, the results actually underestimate the effect of this relationship, because some later cases of successful negotiated agreements are not included in the statistical analyses.

This monograph explores two pathways in which nonviolent resistance during civil war can lead to peace:

1. where nonviolent campaigns aid the negotiated agreement to end civil war that terminates within one year of the end of the armed violence.

2. where nonviolent campaigns first bring about a democratic transition during the civil war, and then the new democratic environment subsequently leads to a peace process and negotiated settlement more than a year after the armed violence ends.

Because the second pathway cannot be considers empirically due to limitations in the data, this is given in-depth consideration through the presentation of the case study of the Alliance for Democracy in Mali, where the agreement was signed after the cessation of violence. This monograph also explores the case of the Second Defiance Campaign in South Africa, which allows us to explore in more detail the first pathway and what is modeled in the statistical analysis. The purpose of these case studies is explored in detail below in Sections 4.4 and 4.5.

4.2. Stage 2: Measuring the Post-Conflict Phase and Democratization

To measure the post-conflict phase that also meets the UCDP threshold, years between the termination of a civil war episode (the first year of inactivity where violence the previous year fell below 25 deaths) and conflict recurrence where a new violent episode emerges has been coded. Between 1955 and 2013, out of the 357 civil war episodes included in this data, a total of 341 were terminated at least a year before 2013. For the post-conflict data analysis, the unit of analysis or data points are 4,141 post-conflict years across the 341 post-conflict periods. These post-conflict years are across 94 post-conflict countries. Again, some countries have multiple periods of post-conflict peace. These periods of peace often fail, followed by conflict recurrence, while some periods of peace continue without conflict recurrence and have stayed peaceful—that is, free of significant armed violence—through 2013 (the last year of the data). As some countries have multiple simultaneous civil wars (e.g., Angola's concurrent rebellions in Cabinda and by UNITA—the National Union for the Total Independence of Angola), this data also explores separate incidents of civil war as different post-conflict periods.

For the analysis of the post-conflict phase this monograph explores two outcomes. First, the recurrence of civil war, and second, post-conflict, long-term democratic transitions. Civil war reoccurs when violence reaches 25 battlefield deaths after previous inactive post-conflict years. This is a dummy measure coded 1 when civil war reoccurs (otherwise 0). Out of 341 post-conflict periods, peace fails in 197 periods and relapses into a new episode of civil war.

The second dependent variable or the result that this monograph wants to explain is instances of post-conflict democratic transitions, coded 1 for democratic transitions (otherwise 0). This data, available from 1955 to 2010, is derived from Ulfelder (2012) who uses various secondary sources to make this categorization. Overall, there are 97 post-conflict periods where the host country transitions to a democracy from an autocracy between 1955 and 2010.

Democratic transitions are less common during active civil war and occur in 35 of the civil war episodes. In the statistical analysis, democratic transitions are explored both: at any timepoint in the post-conflict phase and within a five-year period of the last civil war ending. In order to measure and determine the success of democratic transition, this monograph adopts Ulfelder's definition of a democracy (that he in turn derived from the seminal work of Dahl 1971) as a "form of government in which a free citizenry fairly chooses and routinely holds accountable its rulers" (Ulfelder 2010, 4). For transitions that lead to a successful democratic outcome, four conditions must be satisfied and then sustained to remain a democracy:

■ Rule by elected officials, where policy cannot be vetoed by unelected entities

■ Holding of free and fair elections, free from abuse and deliberate fraud

■ Emergence of an inclusive political system and exercising of equal rights

■ Protection of civil liberties, freedom of speech and assembly.

4.3. Measuring Nonviolent Campaigns and Campaign Attributes

To capture nonviolent campaigns (the main independent or causal variable that this monograph uses to explain results mentioned in previous sections), this monograph adopts campaign-level data on largescale and maximalist nonviolent campaigns from the Nonviolent and Violent Campaigns and Outcome dataset (NAVCO) (Chenoweth and Lewis 2013). This is then aggregated to the country level and merged with data on conflict episodes.

Because the NAVCO data points end in 2006, this data is supplemented with country-level information for 2007–2013 from the Major Episodes of Contention (MEC) dataset taken from Chenoweth and Ulfelder (2017). This provides information on ongoing nonviolent campaigns since 1955, across 170 countries with a minimum population of 500,000. This data provides adequate coverage for 99 countries experiencing episodes of civil war.

Both datasets deploy the same criteria to classify nonviolent campaigns: those which have clear maximalist goals of reform or regime change, are ongoing, and involve at least 1,000 participants in coordinated nonviolent resistance events that occur within one week of one another. This is a dummy measure, where 1 represents a year where an ongoing nonviolent campaign is active within an ongoing civil war (otherwise 0). This variable is lagged by one year, to better ensure that a wartime nonviolent campaign is active and ongoing prior to a civil war being terminated by a peace agreement. Potential issues of endogeneity are discussed in more detail in the statistical analysis below (see Chapter 5).

Propositions 2–8 identified in Chapter 3 outline specific attributes that may increase the likelihood of nonviolent campaigns having a positive impact on peace and post-conflict democratization. This includes social and organizational diversity, leadership structure, and the development of alternative institutions. To measure the specific attributes of these campaigns, data is drawn from the NAVCO 2.1 dataset (Chenoweth and Shay 2017).

The campaign attributes under consideration in this monograph include:

a. **Success of the campaign.** This is a binary variable (only take two values, true or false). A campaign is successful when it has ultimately achieved its primary maximalist goals. Successful campaigns are coded as 1 (otherwise 0).

b. **Number of participants.** This codes the number of participants in six categories, from 1 to 999 participants (lowest category) to more than 1 million (highest category).

c. **Social diversity.** This includes nine binary variables that capture whether the campaign was diverse across nine types of diversity: gender, age, class, urban–rural, ideology, party, regional, ethnicity, and religion. A ratio or score of diversity is also included: the sum of all diversity types, divided by the number of diversity types.

d. **Participation of women.** This is a binary variable that captures whether gender diversity was exhibited in the campaign.

e. **Organizational diversity.** This is the number of organizations involved in the campaign.

f. **Alternative institutions.** This is comprised of two dummy variables: campaign's years where alternative institutions were created, and campaign's years with no alternative institutions. This includes evidence of either parallel educational and social institutions, parallel media, court systems and security structures such as policing.

g. **Campaign leadership structures.** This is comprised of two dummy variables: campaigns with a decentralized leadership, compared to campaigns with hierarchical leadership.[13]

---

13   See the NAVCO 2.1 codebook for more information about these indicators.

When moving to the post-conflict phase (Stage 2), binary variables are created based on whether a nonviolent campaign and the specific campaign attributes were present during the civil war. This assesses the legacy and impact of wartime nonviolent campaigns and specific campaign attributes (a–g) highlighted above on the subsequent post-conflict period.

4.4. Mixed Research Methods Used

This study uses mixed research methods to evaluate the arguments proposed in this monograph, known as a "nested analysis approach" (see Lieberman 2005). This approach combines evidence from data analyses and case study analyses concerning the relationship between nonviolent resistance and the resolution of armed conflict. This study primarily relies on statistical analyses of the data. The findings from these analyses are then compared with findings from two other methods: in and out-of-sample predictive analyses and case study comparisons (George and Bennett 2004).[14] This is to collect evidence for each proposed proposition from three different methodological approaches, thus strengthening the claims made in the monograph.

The mixed methods approach is necessary for this study because active nonviolent campaigns are relatively uncommon in ongoing civil wars, and peace agreements are also relatively rare. Nonviolent campaigns are active in 71 of the 346 civil episodes (20.5%). Only 24 percent of these civil war episodes are terminated through a negotiated agreement (83 out of 346 civil wars). Mixed approaches provide external validity to the evidence provided (from comparing many cases across a large-N sample) and internal validity (in-depth case comparisons). The statistical analysis provides general findings and a blueprint that can then be explored in more depth within the case studies selected below (Lieberman 2005).

4.5. Qualitative Case Studies

This study explores two case studies—South Africa and Mali—in order to further validate the empirical findings (George and Bennett 2004). Specifically, this study explores South Africa's Mass Democracy Campaign (1983–1994) and Mali's March Revolution (1991). These cases were chosen because of the most-different-systems design: the cases are very different, but the outcomes were similar. In each case, a peace settlement and democratization were achieved after a nonviolent movement mobilized during a civil war, with both movements emerging in very difficult contexts: in South Africa, a particularly repressive and sophisticated

---

14   Structured, focused case comparison is used to further explore casual mechanisms to confirm whether findings from a statistical study hold in the selected cases.

26

state security apparatus, and in Mali, within a context of repression, low income, and a low urban population.

Table 5. Key Differences Between the Cases of South Africa and Mali[15]

	PERIOD ANALYZED	REGION	REGIME	INCOME GROUP	% URBAN POPULATION
South Africa (Second Defiance Campaign)	1983–1994	Southern Africa	Single-Party	Upper Middle Income	52.5% (1989)
Mali (Alliance for Democracy)	1991–1996	West Africa	Military Regime	Low Income	23.8% (1991)

While democratization in South Africa formed part of the negotiated agreement that brought about an end to the conflict, in Mali, democratization came first, which subsequently brought about favorable conditions that led to a peace agreement with the Tuareg rebels. As mentioned above, the data on peace agreements is limited in that it only includes negotiated agreements that are signed either during active conflict or the first year after termination. This limitation means that cases such as Mali are missed in the statistical analysis. This will be discussed more when exploring the data in Chapter 5. Despite similar outcomes in Mali and South Africa, these cases differed in terms of the regime type, level of development, urbanization, and the geographical region (see Table 5). Assessing these cases shows that both paths to peace and democratization were possible.

The next chapter tests Propositions 1–8, derived from assumptions in the literature, exploring evidence from the large-N data, followed by the examination of the cases of Mali and South Africa.

---

15   The UCDP classifies two types of civil war: minor civil wars (those that do not reach 1,000 battle-related deaths in a given year) and major civil wars (those that do). Both cases above represent minor civil wars, which may give rise to concerns that this monograph focuses on "easy cases." However, while the civil war is somewhat less intense than other civil war contexts, South Africa and Mali still represent very violent and challenging environments for nonviolent movements to operate within. Moreover, these concerns are not reflected in the data.

First, nonviolent campaigns are proportionally just as likely to occur in major civil wars (39%) than in low-intensity wars (35%). Second, some well-documented successful cases of where wartime nonviolent movements lead to a peace agreement did occur in major civil wars, for instance, Aceh, Nepal, Nicaragua, Palestine, Sierra Leone. Third, these concerns are also not reflected in the statistical analysis. When adding major civil wars into the model, this does not change the findings. While the model shows that major civil wars are less likely to lead to a peace agreement, this is independent of the effect of nonviolent campaigns, which remains positive and statistically significant.

5. Evidence from the Large-N Data

This chapter looks at the data and provides an exploratory statistical analysis of the relationship between nonviolent campaigns, the end of armed conflict, the durability of post-conflict peace, and democratization that might have followed the conflict. This chapter proceeds sequentially: first, exploring the general findings related to negotiated settlements to end the war that take place during ongoing civil war (Stage 1); second, looking into civil war recurrence and democratization in the post-conflict phase (Stage 2).

The first three sections of this chapter discuss the findings presented in Table 6 in greater detail. The fourth and final part of the chapter moves beyond the general findings to explore the impact of specific attributes of nonviolent campaigns on civil war settlements and post-conflict democratization highlighted earlier (points a–g, see page 25).

Overall, the general results strongly support propositions 1a and 1c, derived from existing academic and policy studies presented earlier in Chapter 3 (see Table 6 for the summary).

Table 6. Results of Statistical Analysis: Nonviolent Campaign Attributes and Negotiated Agreements to End Civil War

OUTCOME	EFFECT
Stage 1: Negotiated Settlement to an Ongoing Civil War (P1a)	Nonviolent campaigns had the expected effect; increased the likelihood of negotiated settlements of civil war
Stage 2: Recurrence of Civil War (P1b)	Nonviolent campaigns had no impact on the recurrence of civil war.
Stage 2: Post-Conflict Democratic Transitions (P1c)	Nonviolent campaigns had the expected effect; increased the likelihood of post-conflict democratization.

5.1. Civil War, Nonviolent Campaigns, and Negotiated Agreements

Proposition 1a suggests that nonviolent campaigns lead to civil wars being terminated by a negotiated settlement. On average, the data reveals that a negotiated peace settlement is more likely when nonviolent campaigns are present in the civil war compared to when they are not.

Figure 1 visualizes the average difference; in the years where a civil war was terminated, 32.4 percent of civil war terminations were due to a negotiated agreement when nonviolent campaigns are present, compared to 25.3 percent when they were not.

There are also eight cases where a nonviolent campaign was active and changed the dynamics of ongoing civil war. However, in these eight cases a negotiated settlement is signed more than a year after a civil war ended. For instance, in Niger, the removal of the military regime occurred in 1992, which led to a peace process and eventual agreement with the Tuareg rebels in 1995. If we were to include these eight cases in the data, then the percentage of civil wars ending in a peace settlement increases to 51.4 percent.[16]

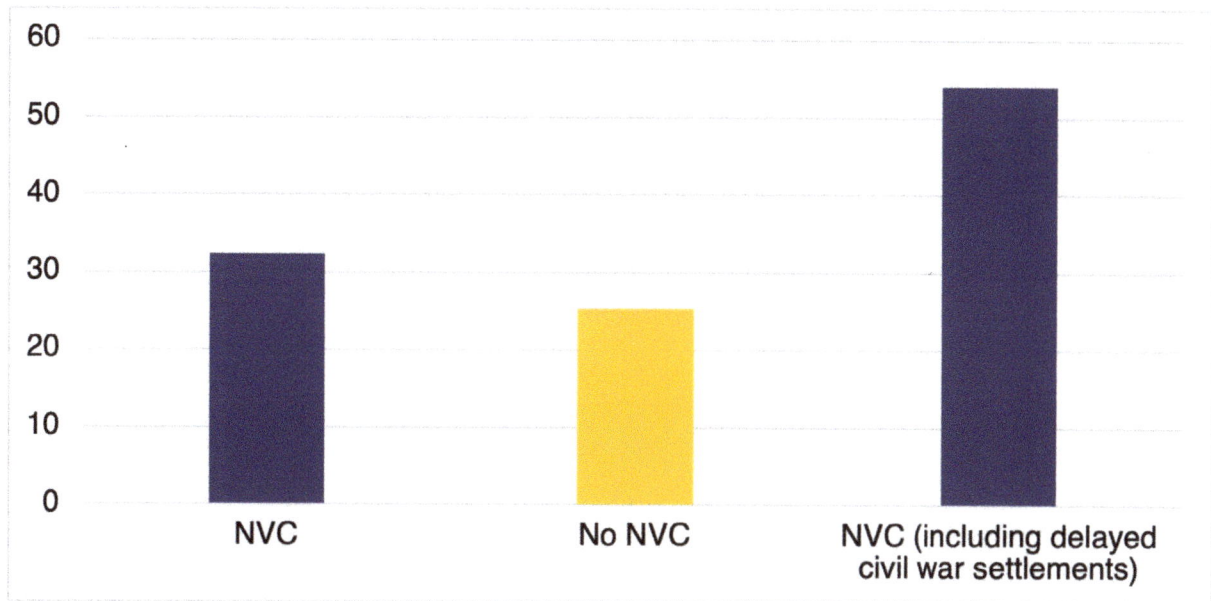

FIGURE 1. Percentage of Civil Wars Ending in a Negotiated Settlement, with and without Nonviolent Resistance Campaign (NVC) in the Final Year of the War (1955–2013)

While the data shows that the presence of nonviolent campaigns during civil wars is more likely to bring about a negotiated agreement, the existence of these campaigns does not always foster conditions for peace. For instance, in the Philippines, the removal of President Marcos has had no concerted impact on the Communist rebellion in the country; in Myanmar, the pro-democracy 8888 campaign led by Aung San Suu Kyi (1988–1990) was violently repressed and had no impact on the various ongoing civil wars in the country; and in Pakistan, the removal of President Musharraf by the Lawyer's Movement did not notably influence the Balochistan armed rebellion in the southwest. In other cases, nonviolent revolution can inadvertently open the space for civil conflict, as was the case in the Iranian revolution. The introduction of the theocratic Iranian regime that emerged in the power vacuum after the

---

16   These cases include Nicaragua, 1978, Bangladesh 1990, Palestine (First Intifada) 1991, Haiti 1991, Niger 1992, Sierra Leone 1996, Papua New Guinea 1997, Aceh 1999. The data on these additional peace agreements that occurred after termination are taken from the PA-X dataset (Bell and Badanjak 2019).

nonviolent uprising led to Kurdish armed rebellion, with the Democratic Party of Iranian Kurdistan (KDPI) demanding democracy.

There are also plausible alternative explanations for the finding displayed in Figure 1. First, it may be that nonviolent movements are simply more common and more likely to emerge in civil war contexts that are already more favorable for peaceful outcomes, for instance, in less autocratic regimes and less repressive contexts (Ritter, 2014; Lehoucq, 2016). These favorable conditions for peace may also explain a greater likelihood of post-conflict democratization. Do nonviolent campaigns simply occur in wartime contexts that are already favorable for negotiated peace settlements?

This does not find support in the analyzed data. Nonviolent movements have the ability to occur in less democratic contexts, including in civil wars. When looking at the average democratic score of countries experiencing civil war—0.335, taken from V-Dem's Polyarchy Score)—nonviolent campaigns more often emerge in less democratic environments (0.322) than this average.[17]

Nonviolent campaigns are also more common in more repressive regimes during periods of civil war. Using the V-Dem's Physical Integrity Score, while the average repression level of regimes that are engaged in civil war is 0.377, nonviolent campaigns are active in more repressive contexts with an average score of 0.388.[18]

In general, the available data shows that nonviolent campaigns are, on average, active in contexts that are in fact less favorable to peace and post-conflict democratization.

Another concern might be that the percentages presented in Figure 1 only represent a snapshot of the data. It is not clear whether this reported average is merely a coincidence. After all, this statistical outcome may have occurred simply by chance. This necessitates the use of more robust statistical methods, namely regression analysis.

While familiar to most scholars and practitioners, logistic regression is a form of statistical analysis for binary outcomes (was there a peace agreement or not), which specifically explores whether a relationship has occurred by chance—whether civil war situations where nonviolent campaigns are present are indeed statistically different from those without these campaigns)—while controlling for other factors that may explain this relationship.[19]

---

17   This scale ranges from 0 (least democratic) to 1 (most democratic). See Appendix I for a more detailed explanation of this data.

18   Again, this is a scale from 0 (least repressive) and 1 (most repressive). Physical integrity is understood as freedom from political killings and torture by the government. Please refer to Appendix I for a more detailed explanation of this data.

19   See Chapters 9 and 10 and the appendix for a more detailed explanation of how the regression models work, the statistical controls used in these models and the full statistical results.

Table 7. A Note on Interpreting Predicted Probabilities

Many graphs in this monograph refer to predicted probabilities. A predicted probability is based on regression analysis of past cases, and it forecasts the likelihood of an outcome for each case, given all the factors that are included in the regression model (known as in-sample prediction). In this monograph, a predicted probability is based on the likelihood of a mutually exclusive event occurring (i.e., peace occurs or does not occur) and is the averaged predicted probability across all cases.

For example, Figure 2 (on the following page) is based on data that shows that from 1955 to 2013 negotiated agreements occurred in only 85 out of 1,798 armed conflict episode years—meaning 4.7 percent of armed conflicts actually ended in a negotiated settlement. Using the logistic regression model, I can calculate the probability of an armed conflict ending in a negotiated settlement for cases for where nonviolent campaigns were present, and then compare this with the calculated probability of negotiated agreements in cases where nonviolent campaigns were not present. These predictions are not actual outcomes, but rather predicted outcomes based on the regression model that controls for various factors that influenced the outcome (for example, the presence of mediation, peacekeeping, and the intensity of the conflict—that is, numbers of battlefield deaths). The result is a predicted probability of 6 percent that a violent conflict will achieve a negotiated settlement when a nonviolent campaign is present, and a 2 percent predicted probability that such an outcome will happen in the absence of a nonviolent campaign. This means that the presence of a nonviolent campaign increases the likelihood of a negotiated settlement by 200 percent, as compared to when a nonviolent campaign is absent.

Overall, the regression results report a positive and statistically significant relationship, meaning that nonviolent campaigns do, independently of other factors, increase the likelihood of civil war settlements. Furthermore, we are more than 95 percent confident (the accepted academia threshold for a high degree of confidence) that this relationship has not simply occurred by chance, even when controlling for other variables that account for rival explanations.[20]

Protests may occur *because* of the peace process, both in the form of anti and pro-government protests. Peace agreements can create space for nonviolent resistance as well as generate new grievances for mobilization, as seen recently in Colombia. However, such possibility is simply not evident in the data. In all the models looking at peace agreements, wartime nonviolent campaigns are lagged by one year, meaning anti-government nonviolent campaigns are already mobilized and ongoing prior to a civil war that is terminated by a peace agreement. Moreover, case evidence also suggests that nonviolent campaigns come first, and as Figure 1 shows, in some cases there is a significant temporal lag between a nonviolent campaign emerging and a peace process that ends in an agreement occurring only later.

---

20   See Model 2 from Figure 15 in the regression analysis—see Appendix II. Figures 16–17 show how predictive non-violent campaigns are of peace settlements in comparison to third-party mediation.

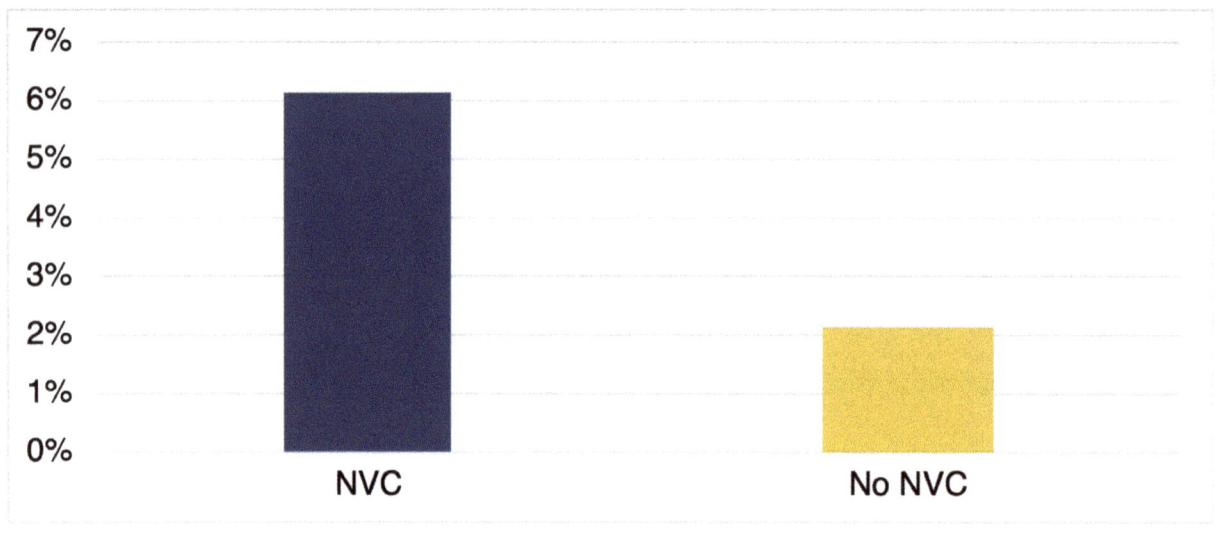

FIGURE 2. Nonviolent Campaign (NVC) and the Predicted Probability
of a Negotiated Settlement, based on data from 1955 to 2013

Figure 2 visualizes the predictions from this regression analysis, providing the clearest and most meaningful way to present the findings from various analyses conducted in this monograph.[21] On the y-axis is the predicted likelihood of a negotiated agreement, while on the x-axis is the predicted probability of a negotiated agreement where nonviolent campaigns are present, compared to cases where nonviolent campaigns are absent.

These results show that between 1955 and 2013, negotiated agreements were three times more likely to occur when nonviolent campaigns were present during a civil war, compared to civil war episodes where nonviolent campaigns were absent, keeping constant other key explanations including favorable conditions for peace, such as mediation, peacekeeping, and lower numbers of battlefield deaths (i.e., less intensity). The independent effects of nonviolent campaigns on negotiated settlements during civil wars are substantial; even though the probability of a peace agreement is quite low (negotiated agreements occurred in only 85 out of 1,798 violent conflict episode years).

Statistical analysis was also performed to explore the relationship between nonviolent campaigns during civil war and the likelihood of negotiated agreements over the duration of the violent conflict, using a survival duration model. This models how long peace is

---

21   It is conventional to report predictions alongside regression outputs when using a binary outcome (e.g., there was an agreement or there was not an agreement). This is because it is not possible to directly interpret estimates (the coefficient) from logit regression models that are used to explore binary outcomes. While the coefficients from this model tell us whether the relationship is positive or negative, unlike the predictions, this does not tell us the magnitude of the effect.

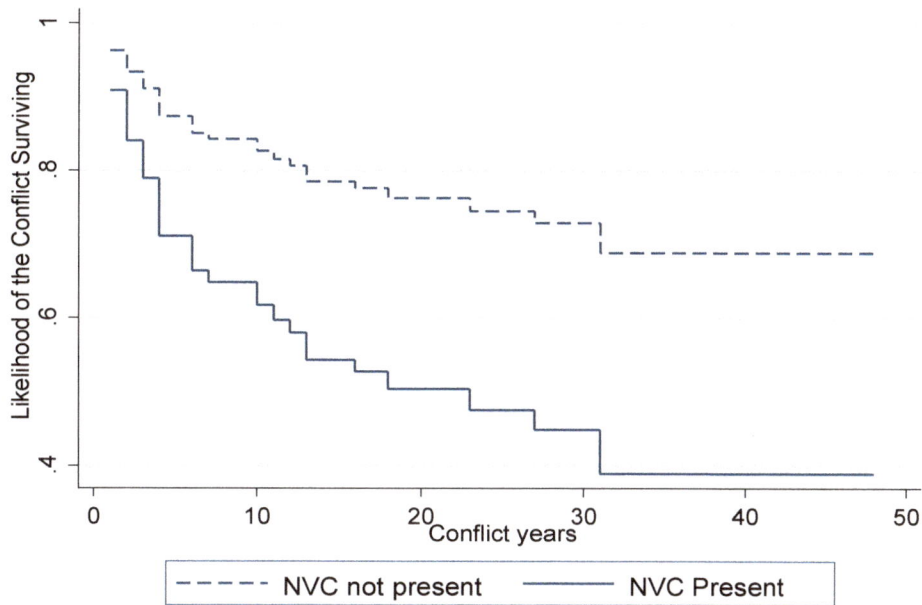

FIGURE 3. Nonviolent Campaign (NVC) and the Duration of Civil War (1955–2013)[22]

maintained or survives before conflict reoccurrence interrupts this timeline. Figure 3 visualizes the likelihood of civil war "surviving" on the y-axis and the number of civil war episodes' years on the x-axis. At all stages of the lifecycle in all civil wars in the data, the likelihood of the violent conflict continuing is substantially reduced when largescale nonviolent campaigns are present within the conflict. For instance, after 5 years of civil war, a peace agreement is around 25 percent more likely when nonviolent campaigns are present compared to when they are not.

Another possibility is that nonviolent campaigns may aid the termination of civil war but not necessarily negotiated agreements per se. There are other ways in which a civil war can end, such as a rebel victory, a military victory, or low activity. If theoretical assumptions are correct, the effect of wartime nonviolent movements should only be isolated to outcomes where a settlement is agreed. Furthermore, if wartime nonviolent campaigns weaken governmental power vis-à-vis the rebels, then the rebels might calculate that there is less incentive to seek peace. In other words, with a weakened government, the rebels could sense the opportunity to win through military means, aiding rebel victory rather than a peaceful settlement.

22   See Appendix II, based on Model 4 from Figure 15.

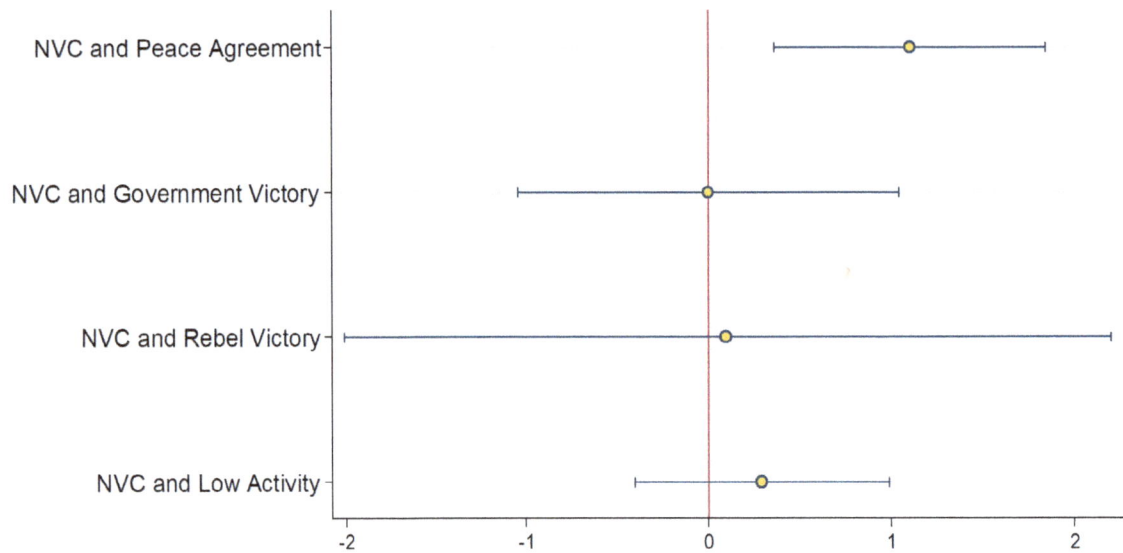

FIGURE 4. Nonviolent Campaigns (NVC)
and Types of Civil War Termination (1955–2013)

Figure 4 displays the results from the statistical analysis of civil war outcomes. This model, known as multinomial regression, generalizes logistic regression to multiple categories—the different types of civil war termination. As the results show, nonviolent campaigns during civil war increases only the likelihood of peace agreements, not civil war terminations by other means. Here there is no evidence nonviolent movements aid rebel victory.

5.2. The Legacy of Nonviolent Campaigns and the Recurrence of Armed Conflict

Moving beyond civil war, the analysis now turns to the post-conflict phase, the intermediate peace years that fall between the first year of peace following the end of a civil war and the year in which conflict reoccurs (or does not reoccur) prior to 2013. This chapter first explores the relationship between nonviolent campaigns that are present in the previous civil war and the recurrence of civil war in post-conflict periods. **Proposition 1b** suggests that the activities of nonviolent campaigns during civil war increase post-conflict durability of peace. The data however shows no such effect.

Figure 5 shows that the predictions from the regression model reveal no notable effect. There is no significant difference between the predicted likelihood of conflict recurrence, given the presence or absence of nonviolent campaigns in the preceding civil war.[23] These predictions take into account possible alternative explanations such as the intensity and length of the previous civil war and the current level of GDP and democracy within a post-conflict state. Nonviolent campaigns during civil war have no impact on civil war recurrence,

---

23   See Appendix II, based on the final model from Figure 18.

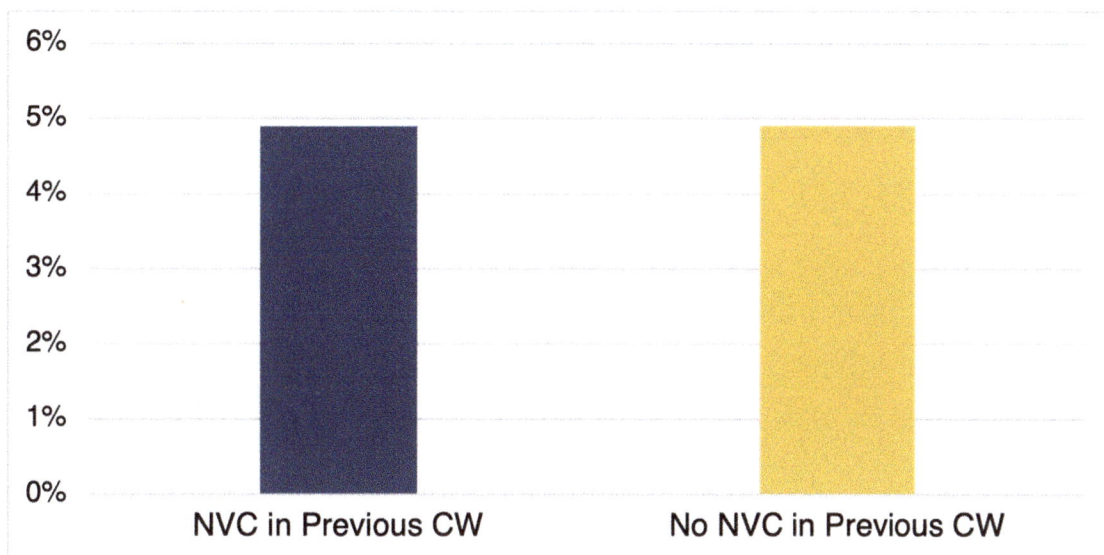

FIGURE 5. Predicted Probability of Civil War Recurrence, based on data from 1955 to 2013

regardless how the earlier civil war was terminated—whether by negotiated settlement or exhaustion of violence—and irrespective of the success of nonviolent campaigns.

This finding is somewhat contradictory to findings in earlier works. Yet, while Chenoweth and Stephan (2011) find that nonviolent campaigns reduce the likelihood of future outbreaks of civil war, unlike this study, their analysis is not conducted solely on a harder set of cases where a country has a recent history of civil war. One of the strongest determinants of conflict recurrence is a previous history of civil war. Countries without a history of civil war are much less prone to a subsequent war. The inclusion of countries without a history of civil war may explain the positive results in Chenoweth and Stephan's (2011) large-N analysis.[24]

This monograph does not suggest that the legacy of nonviolent campaigns during civil war has no impact on the post-conflict phase. The process of civil war relapse is very complex. While nonviolent movements are able to emerge in civil wars, the root causes of civil war are very difficult to resolve. For one, war-prone states tend to be institutionally weaker and resource deprived. It is difficult for states with history of civil war to escape the recurrence of violent conflict even when attempting to democratize, as they often lack the resources to build stable institutions that can prevent future violence. Moreover, while this study has shown that wartime nonviolent movements are positively associated with negotiated settlements, some literature on conflict recurrence finds that civil wars that end in victory are less prone

---

24   Another key determinant of civil war often included in the literature is country GDP. Lower GDP and a history of war keep countries in what is known as the conflict trap; continued episodes of civil war destabilize already weak economies which in turn risks further conflict (see Collier et al. 2003).

to relapse than those ended by an agreement, as it significantly restrains the capacity of the losers to rearm and renew combat (Quinn, Mason, and Gurses 2007; Kreutz 2010).

The next section of this chapter proceeds to the next inquiry of this monograph: whether the legacy of nonviolent campaigns increases the likelihood of democratization after the end of civil war.

5.3. Nonviolent Campaigns in Civil Wars and the Prospect of Democratization After the End of Civil War

Proposition 1c is based on the assumption that nonviolent campaigns that emerged during civil wars increase the likelihood of post-conflict democratization. Due to data availability on democratic transitions, the analysis assesses this proposition by exploring the period between 1955 and 2010 (not 2013) where data is available. What does the data say about post-conflict democratization and nonviolent movements after the end of a civil war?

First, the data provides clear evidence that wartime nonviolent campaigns have a substantial and positive effect on post-conflict democratization. This is particularly the case within a five-year period following the end of the previous civil war and after a negotiated settlement has been signed—democratization and power sharing is often part of the agreement between warring actors.

Not only do nonviolent campaigns tend to emerge in difficult and less democratic wartime environments, but they are also associated with more democratic post-conflict periods. The average democratic score for post-conflict countries where nonviolent campaigns were active during the civil war that ended is 0.499—Nigeria in 2000 or Bangaladesh in 1992 after their democratic transitions—compared to 0.336—Yemen in the mid-1990s—in post-conflict states where they were not active (based on the V-Dem Polyarchy Score). To put this in perspective, most observers would consider democracies to have a score of at least 0.6, with those closer to 1 being the most democratic. In other words, post-conflict countries are much closer to this democratic threshold when nonviolent campaigns are active during the war.

Within a five-year period after the termination of a civil war, a democratic transition occurs in 14 percent of cases when a nonviolent campaign is present. Conversely, such a democratic transition is three times less likely (4.8% of cases) when civil resistance is not present.

The long-term impact of a nonviolent movement that occurred during a civil war does not always guarantee democratization after the end of the violent conflict, as the likelihood of post-conflict democratization is still relatively low. Nevertheless, there are prominent cases of post-conflict democratization that followed a civil war in which nonviolent campaigns were present and played a significant role.

For example, in South Africa, the Second Defiance Campaign (1983–1994) helped to push for peace talks and eventually South Africa's transition from apartheid dictatorship into multiparty politics. Liberia's transition to democracy in 2006 came after the Women of Liberia Mass Action for Peace helped to end the civil war in 2003, in which the country's first female president was elected. In East Timor, the Timorese Independence Campaign had an important legacy on the civil war and eventual secession from Indonesia, leading to a democratic transition in 2002 in the new East Timor state, three years after the peace agreement was signed with Indonesia.

There have also been numerous cases in which nonviolent campaigns during civil war successfully led a democratic transition, which then subsequently laid the foundations for a peace process, and culminating in a comprehensive agreement ending violent conflict signed a few years after democratization began. While this is difficult to capture statistically, due to the limitations in the data, there are numerous examples where this has occurred.

One of the relevant cases explored in detail in Chapter 6 is Mali. In 1991 the Alliance for Democracy removed the military regime and initiated a democratic transition. This laid the foundations for meaningful talks with the Tuareg rebels and eventually, in 1995, an agreement to end violence. A similar trend was seen in neighboring Niger, where the removal of the military regime in 1992 led to a peace agreement with Niger's Tuareg rebels in 1994. In Bangladesh, the successful pro-democracy campaign (1987–1990) brought about democratization that reinvigorated the peace process around the Chittagong rebellion. The full agreement was signed later in 1997.

While the statistical analysis only captures post-conflict democratization, and not democratization that occurs before the negotiations that produce an agreement, the regression results also provide robust evidence that nonviolent campaigns that are active during civil war increase the likelihood of post-conflict democratization, in line with the statistical averages reported above.

Based on these regression analyses,[25] Figure 6 visualizes the probability of post-conflict democratization (y-axis) when nonviolent movements are present during civil war and when they are absent (x-axis). This shows that post-conflict democratization, while comparably rare, is more than twice as likely to occur when nonviolent campaigns are present in a civil war, as opposed to their absence.

---

25 See Appendix II, based on the first model from Figure 19. The predictive analysis in Appendix II shows that the existence of mediation in the previous civil war and a greater number of democratic neighbors are greater predictors of post-conflict democratization than the presence of nonviolent campaigns in the last civil war. However, these effects are independent of one another—i.e., the presence of mediation or more democratic neighbors does not undermine the impact of nonviolent campaigns on post-conflict democracy.

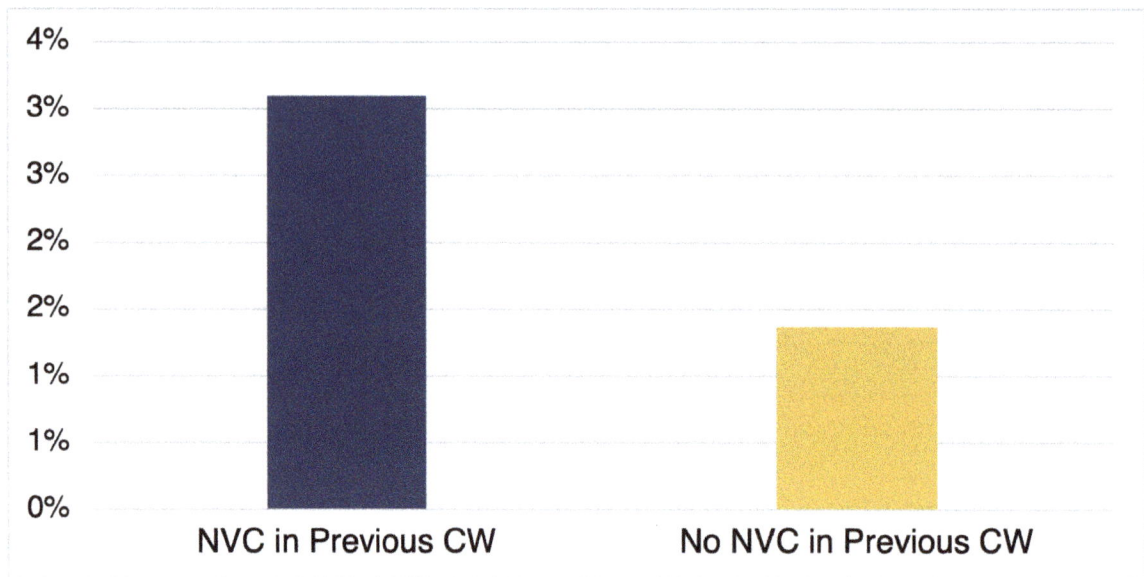

FIGURE 6. Nonviolent Campaigns (NVC) and the Predicted Probability
of Democratization after a Civil War, based on data from 1955 to 2010

Figure 7 shows that nonviolent campaigns that were present during a civil war that ended with a negotiated agreement brought about higher level of democratization in the five-year period after the end of the civil war.[26] The left graph shows that democratization is over four times more likely to occur within five years after the end of civil war when nonviolent movements were present in civil war compared to cases where such movements did not happen.

The right graph shows that democratization after a civil war is six times more likely when following a peace agreement, and where nonviolent campaigns were present in comparison when they both were absent. And what was an independent impact of negotiated agreement? How much force does it offer toward democratization in comparison with nonviolent movement? Again, the effects of nonviolent campaigns are measured independently of other explanations in the regression models.

---

26   See full results in Appendix II, Figure 19.

38

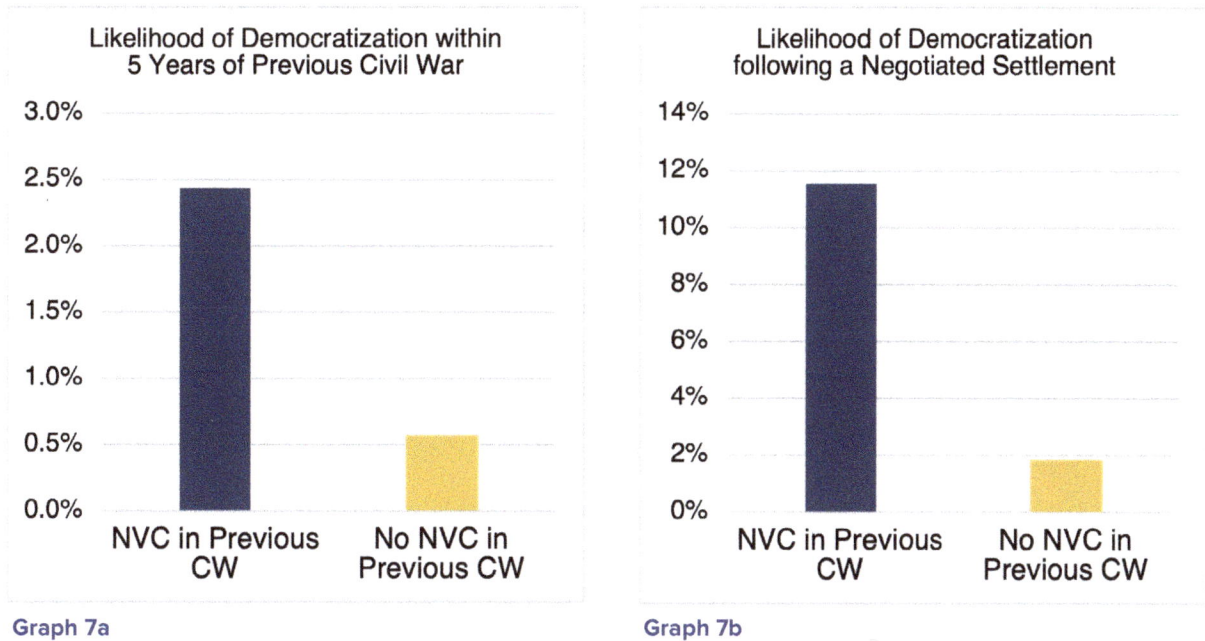

Likelihood of Democratization within
5 Years of Previous Civil War

Graph 7a

Likelihood of Democratization
following a Negotiated Settlement

Graph 7b

FIGURE 7. Nonviolent Campaigns (NVC) and Predicted Probabilities for Specific Contexts
of Post-Conflict Democratization, based on data from 1955 to 2010

The findings so far have shown that nonviolent campaigns present during civil war can both aid negotiated settlements to civil wars and help subsequent democratization. In Appendix II, additional quantitative approaches are deployed that provide further evidence that corroborate these findings (see Figure 21). The final part of this chapter explores what specific campaign features help to explain the positive trends between nonviolent resistance, negotiated civil war settlements, and post-conflict democratization.

5.4. Campaigns Attributes, Negotiated Settlements, and Post-Conflict Democratization

The analyses below focus on negotiated agreements and post-conflict democratization in the context of specific campaign attributes. This study excludes the inquiry about the impact of specific campaign attributes on conflict recurrence because no evidence is found linking nonviolent campaigns and their attributes with a relapse of civil war. These non-findings are discussed in more details in Appendix II.

Assumptions derived for the purpose of this study (presented in Chapter 3) suggest that the following features of nonviolent campaigns might help explain why post-conflict democratization and negotiated agreements to end civil war are more likely.

- **Success of the campaign** (P2a and P2c): A negotiated settlement and a post-conflict democratic transition should be more likely when a wartime nonviolent campaign has been successful in achieving political change.

- **Greater number of participants** (P3a and P3c): This provides a movement with more leverage against the violent government and the ability to pressure for political change.

- **Greater social diversity** (P4a and P4c): More diversity within a campaign allows a movement to exercise different pressure points on the repressive government to force political change, and it promotes inclusive and democratic principles.

- **Participation of women** (P5a and P5c): The participation of women in nonviolent movements further lowers barriers to participation and is more likely to elicit loyalty shifts. Women's participation can also promote genuine women's empowerment that can be integrated into the peace process and lead to a more inclusive post-conflict society.

- **More organizational diversity** (P6a and P6c): The coalition building required to form a nonviolent movement can provide a blueprint for power sharing and democratization.

- **The creation of alternative institutions** (P7a and P7c): Independent parallel institutions shift power away from the state toward organized community and thus undermine the legitimacy of the state and support the design of inclusive democratic institutions.

- **A decentralized campaign and its leadership structure** (P8a and P8c): This distributes ownership for the campaign to a large and diverse group of people, which may render it more resilient and thus adaptable to violent contexts. This also makes a movement more likely to promote democratic principles of sharing power than a centralized nonviolent movement.

The discussion below explores these assumptions in relation to negotiated settlements using the same statistical regression analyses and statistical controls as the previous chapters. This follows sequentially, exploring each proposition (from 2 through 8), in relation to negotiated agreements, and then in relation to post-conflict democratization.

Impact of Attributes of Nonviolent Campaigns on Negotiated Agreements (Stage 1)

The data and findings from the statistical analyses suggest that the success of nonviolent campaigns, a greater number of participants, greater social diversity, a more decentralized leadership, and the existence of alternative institutions all help to explain why nonviolent campaigns during civil war may increase the likelihood of negotiated agreements to end the war. This finding lends support to Propositions 2a–5a and 7a–8a (see Table 8).

However, in the regression analysis, no support is found for Proposition 6a; a higher number of civil society organizations within a nonviolent campaign is not associated with an increased likelihood of negotiated settlement (see Appendix II for a full discussion of the results, Figures 21–25). To visualize these results, the next paragraphs will explore the predictions from the regression analysis, going through each proposition sequentially.

Table 8. Nonviolent Campaign Attributes and Negotiated Settlements to Civil War

Success of the campaign (P2a)	Had the expected effect. Negotiated agreements are most likely in cases where nonviolent campaigns successfully achieved their goals during a civil war.
Greater number of participants (P3a)	Had the expected effect. Larger nonviolent campaigns during civil war are positively associated with negotiated settlements.
Greater social diversity (P4a)	Had the expected and strong effect. Negotiated settlements are most likely in cases where nonviolent campaign participants derive from a greater number of social groups.
Participation of women (P5a)	Had the expected effect. The participation of women in nonviolent campaigns during civil war increases the likelihood of a negotiated settlement.
More organizational diversity (P6a)	No measurable effect. Organizational diversity had positive effects on negotiated settlements in South Africa (i.e., allowed a diverse leadership that was adaptable to state repression, allowing the movement to continue to pressure for a negotiated end to apartheid and the armed conflict—see Chapter 6). However, this is not evident in other cases, where organizational diversity may create disunity and divisions can undermine the campaign.
Creation of alternative institutions (P7a)	Had the expected effect. Nonviolent campaigns that create alternative institutions during civil war are more positively associated with negotiated settlements than campaigns that do not.
A decentralized leadership structure (P8a)	Had the expected and strong effect. Decentralized nonviolent campaigns are consistently associated with negotiated agreement to civil war.

The Success and Size of a Campaign and Negotiated Settlements to Civil War

Starting with the success and size (number of participants) of wartime nonviolent campaigns (Figure 8), Graph 8a visualizes the probability of a civil war negotiated agreement (y-axis), comparing contexts where these campaign attributes are present or absent (x-axis). The predictions show that nonviolent campaigns that are successful in achieving their maximalist political aims are more than twice as likely to lead to peace settlements than campaigns that fail to achieve their aims.[27]

---

27   See Appendix II, based on the first model from Figure 22.

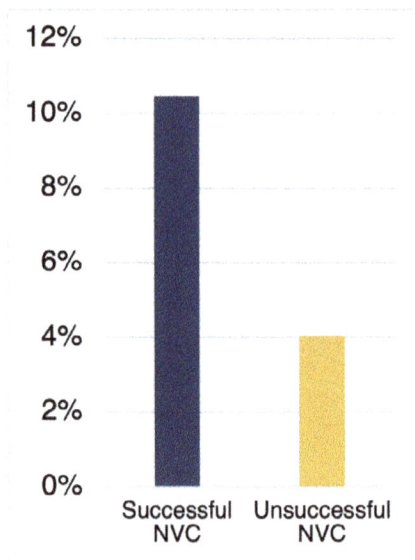

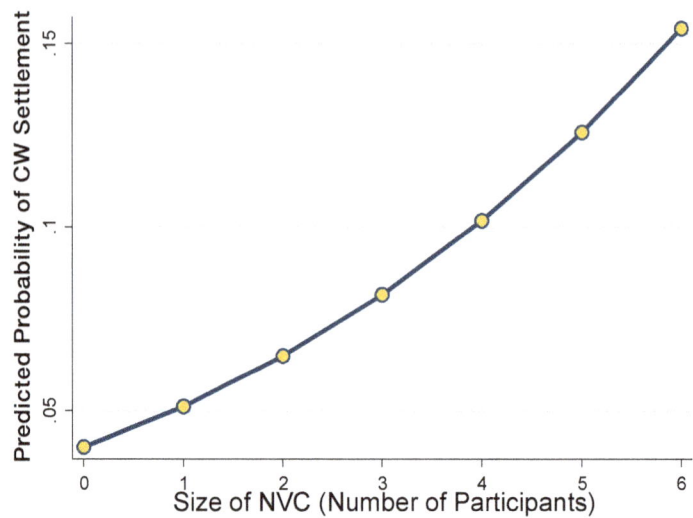

Graph 8a

Graph 8b

FIGURE 8. Success and Size of Nonviolent Campaigns (NVC)
and Civil War Settlements, based on data from 1955 to 2013

Graph 8b then explores the predicted likelihood of negotiated settlement (y-axis), given the size of the wartime nonviolent campaign (x-axis). The line plots the average predicted effect, which increases as the size of the campaign increases. In other words, *the likelihood of a peaceful settlement is higher in cases where wartime nonviolent campaigns have more participants.* The Second Defiance Campaign in South Africa represents an illustrative case. The campaign eventually led to negotiations to end the apartheid regime and the conflict. The campaign peaked at around 4 million participants and averaged around 1.8 million between 1984 and 1994 and was successful in bringing about regime change.

Social, Organizational, and Gender Diversity of Campaigns and Negotiated Settlements

Moving to social and organizational diversity of wartime nonviolent campaigns, Figure 9a demonstrates that socially diverse participation in campaigns is an important predictor of peaceful settlements to civil war. Graph 9a visualizes the predicted likelihood of negotiated settlements to civil war (y-axis), given the level of social diversity of participants within a campaign (x-axis).[28] This explores the level of diversity using a ratio based on NAVCO's data (it calculates how many forms of diversity a campaign possesses and then divides this by the nine forms of diversity).[29] Graph 9b shows that as part of this diversity, women's participation in the

---

28   See Appendix II, based on models from Figure 22.

29   The nine types of social diversity are: gender, age, class, urban–rural, ideology, party, regional, ethnicity, and religion.

movement is particularly important; the likelihood of a negotiated agreement is twice as likely when movements are gender diverse, compared to campaigns that are not gender diverse.

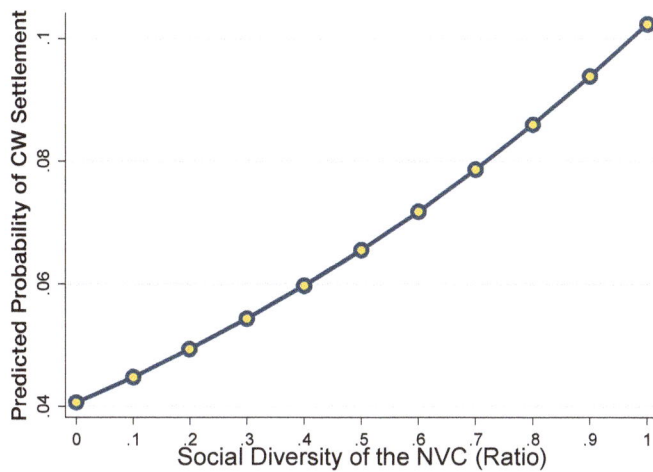

Graph 9a

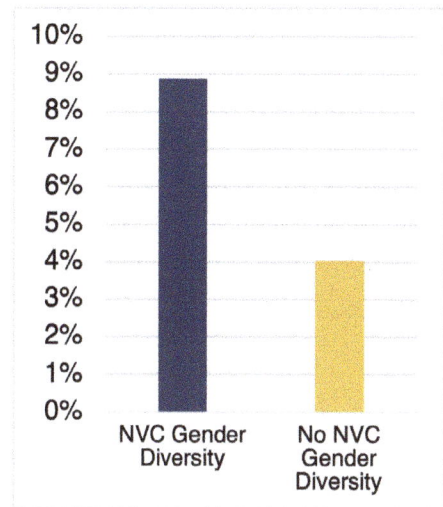

Graph 9b

FIGURE 9. Social Diversity, Women's Participation, and Civil War Settlements, based on data from 1955 to 2013

The line in Graph 9a plots the average predicted effect and shows an upward trend in the relationship between the social diversity of a nonviolent movement and the likelihood of a negotiated settlement. The more socially diverse a wartime nonviolent campaign is, the more likely the civil war will be terminated through negotiated settlement.

Greater social diversity in campaigns has been shown to be crucial in forcing government concessions (Chenoweth and Stephan 2011). In the context of civil war, this also appears to be important. In many cases social diversity transcends the conflict divisions. For instance, in Sierra Leone in 1996, nonviolent resistance against the government included students, lawyers, and women's groups who came from various ethnic groups. The Second Defiance Campaign in South Africa was not only large but also incredibly diverse, representing men and women from different classes, ideologies, regions, ethnicities, and urban and rural areas. More diverse campaigns are not only better placed to pressure for change, but also promote coalition building between groups, which can support peace processes and reconciliation.

Going beyond individual participants and looking at the numbers of organizations within a nonviolent movement, there is no clear effect. The regression results report a positive estimate, but this is not statistically significant. Therefore, while there are a few cases where a greater number of civil society organizations is positively associated with the negotiated agreements to civil war, this is offset by a majority of cases where greater organizational diversity had very little effect.[30] In South Africa, greater organizational diversity had a huge impact on ushering in the peace process that brought an end to apartheid and the armed conflict. Organizational diversity provided the movement with a diverse leadership, which was important because it allowed the movement to adapt to state repression. When the state and security forces targeted one organization, another organization within the movement stepped into the leadership role, keeping sustained pressure on the regime (see Chapter 6). In other contexts, such organizational diversity creates disunity and divisions between organizations, which instead undermine the campaign, reflecting what Pinckney, Butcher, and Braithwaite (2019) call the "diversity dilemma" in regard to the organizational roots of a nonviolent movement.

Cases where peaceful settlements were not achieved despite the organizational diversity of a nonviolent movement include Haiti in 2004, where the anti-Aristide protests, although representing various organizations, did not lead to a peace process that would end the National Liberation and Reconstruction Front–led armed uprising. In Bangladesh in 2007, while the Awami League protests were successful in removing the government and represented more than ten organizations across Bangladeshi civil society, this nonviolent uprising had no impact on the PBCP (Janajuddha) Maoist rebellion. This echoes the People Power nonviolent uprising in the Philippines, a movement that successfully removed the highly repressive Marcos regime in 1986, and represented a diverse array of Filipino organizations, yet had no impact on the ongoing Communist rebellion.

This contrasts with the case of Nepal, where opposition parties and organizations collaborated with the Communist Party of Nepal (CPNM) that abandoned the armed rebellion to join the April Uprising, whose eventual success led to the peace agreement. Another well know case is South Africa's Second Defiance Campaign (1983–94), where organizational diversity was key in allowing the movement to adapt to state repression and paved the way for the peace process. This further justifies the need to explore specific case studies to further assess this non-finding in the data. The cases of South Africa and another illustrative case, Mali's March Revolution (1990–92), are explored in Chapter 6, specifically highlighting the vital importance of both social and organizational diversity.

Campaign Leadership Structure, Alternative Institutions, and Negotiated Settlements

The importance of organizational diversity may differ in other campaigns as noted by the regression analyses, and may depend on other attributes of the campaign, namely that diverse movements appear to be most effective because they tend to have a decentralized leadership. The regression results show that the most important attribute of wartime

---

30   See Appendix II, based on models from Figure 23.

nonviolent campaign seems to be a decentralized leadership structure, as it appears to have the strongest substantive effect (see Figure 10, graph 10a).[31]

The predictions from the statistical analyses show that civil wars are 2.5 times more likely to end in a negotiated agreement when decentralized nonviolent campaigns are present, compared to hierarchical nonviolent campaigns.

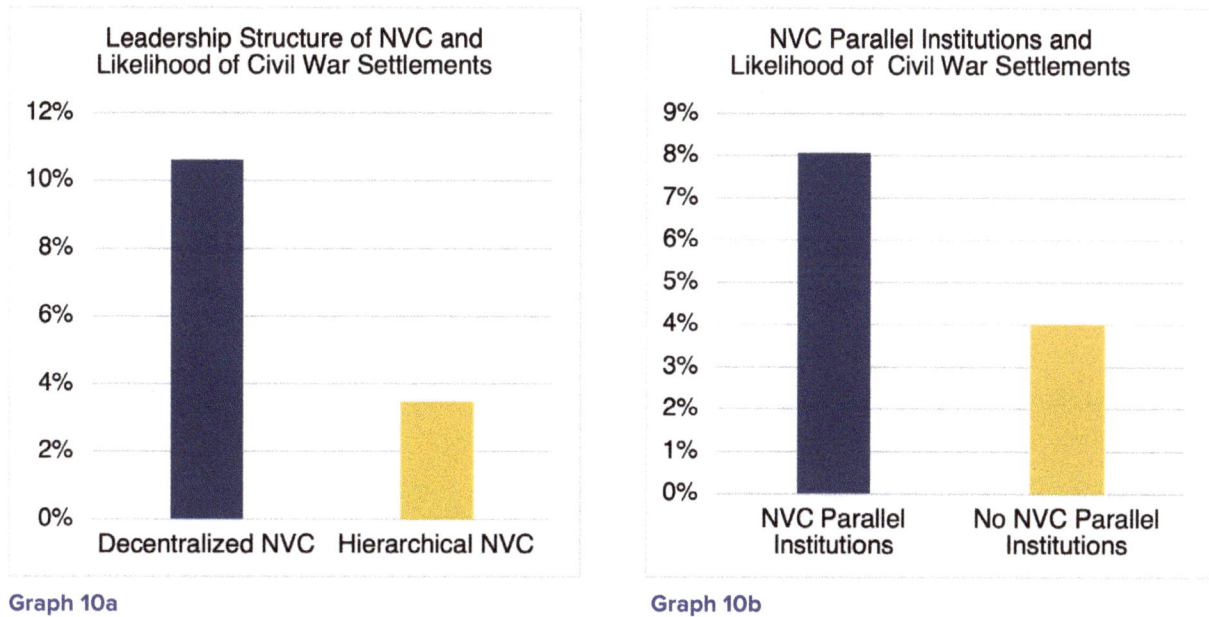

Graph 10a

Graph 10b

FIGURE 10. Leadership Structure and Parallel Institutions of Nonviolent Campaigns (NVC) and Predicted Probability of Civil War Settlements, based on data from 1955 to 2013

In the cases of Mali and South Africa, this was a hugely important attribute that helped these nonviolent campaigns adapt, survive, and resurge despite state violence. Shared and dispersed leadership also provides an important blueprint for the peace process and negotiations for power sharing, as it increases ownership of the process among many stakeholders and shows how the power could be shared effectively. Beyond Mali and South Africa, there are numerous examples where decentralized campaigns led to an agreement to end civil war, from the well-known cases of Nepal and Palestine (First Intifada) to Niger and Nicaragua.

The final campaign attribute explored here is the establishment of alternative institutions (see Graph 10b). Alternative institutions are often formed by nonviolent campaigns to counter state institutions that may be inefficient or simply discriminatory. Alternative institutions, such as parallel education and governance systems, are self-sufficient and based on grassroots activities that can promote inclusivity. These activities can support a peace process and

---

31   Also based on models from Figure 23 in Appendix II.

provide a blueprint for peace talks, building on the creative and inclusive experience of developing these parallel institutions and their subsequent work.

The predictions show that civil wars where a wartime nonviolent campaign develops parallel institutions are twice as likely to result in a negotiated settlement compared to cases where nonviolent movements do not create parallel institutions.[32] The next section of this chapter explores the legacy of the same attributes in relation to post-conflict democratization.

Impact of Nonviolent Campaign Attributes on Post-Conflict Democratization (Stage 2)

This section explores the legacy of specific nonviolent campaign attributes, and how types of nonviolent campaigns taking place during civil war influence democratization after the end of civil war (Figures 11–13). The results are similar to the impact nonviolent campaigns have during civil war (presented earlier in Figures 8–10).

All campaign attributes appear to be important; larger, successful, greater social and organizational diversity, decentralized leadership, and parallel institutions within nonviolent movements all have an individual positive impact on subsequent democratization (see Table 9).

Table 9. Nonviolent Campaign Attributes and Post-Conflict Democratization (1955–2010)

Success of the campaign (P2c)	Had the expected strong effect. Post-conflict democratization is much more likely when wartime nonviolent campaigns successfully achieved their goals.
Greater number of participants (P3c)	Had the expected strong effect. Larger wartime nonviolent campaigns are an important predictor of post-conflict democratization.
Greater social diversity (P4c)	Had the expected effect. Nonviolent campaigns during civil war that are more socially diverse increase the likelihood of post-conflict democratization.
Participation of women (P5c)	Had the expected effect. Nonviolent campaigns during civil war that include the participation of women increase the likelihood of post-conflict democratization.
More organizational diversity (P6c)	Had the expected strong effect. A greater number of organizations, and the coalition building this requires, positively impact post-conflict democratization.
Creation of alternative institutions (P7c)	Had the expected effect. Wartime nonviolent campaigns with alternative institutions are associated with post-conflict democratization, albeit the effect is weaker than above.
A decentralized leadership structure (P8c)	Had the expected effect. Decentralized nonviolent campaigns increase the likelihood of democratization after the civil war.

---

32   See Appendix II - based on models from figure 24

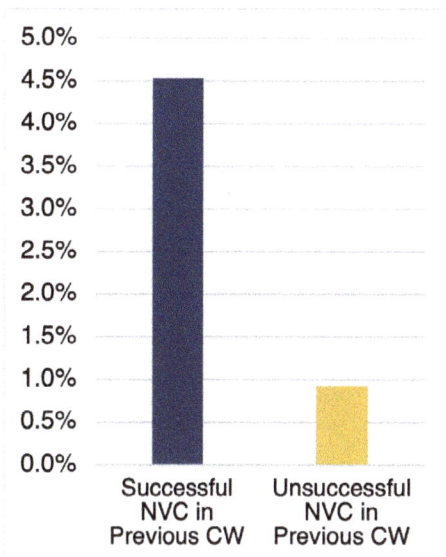

Graph 11a

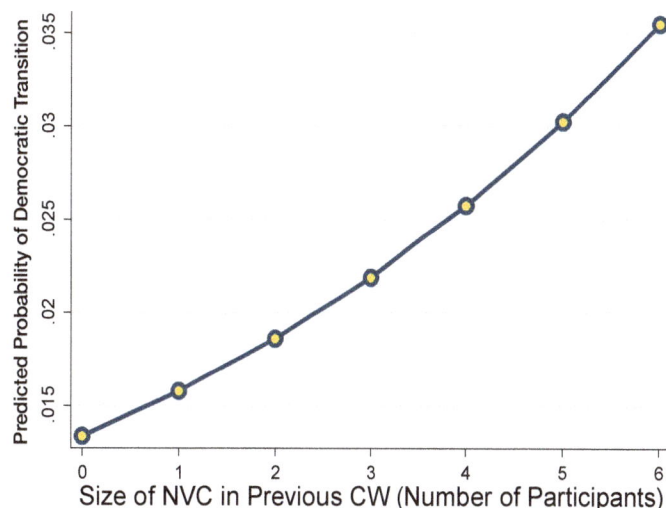

Graph 11b

FIGURE 11. Success and Size of Wartime Nonviolent Campaigns (NVC) and Post-Conflict Democratization, based on data from 1955 to 2010

The Success and Size of a Campaign and Post-Conflict Democratization

Starting with the success and size of nonviolent campaigns during civil war, Figure 11 visualizes the predicted likelihood of post-conflict democratization given the presence of these two attributes.[33] Graph 11a shows that the legacy of successful nonviolent campaigns is crucial in explaining subsequent post-conflict democratization.

Successful campaigns are nearly five times more likely to bring about democratization after the end of civil war than unsuccessful campaigns. By removing undemocratic regimes or forcing concessions, nonviolent movements lay the foundations for subsequent democratization, often included as part of a negotiated peace process. The size of the nonviolent campaign (a key predictor of successful campaigns) is associated with a greater likelihood of post-conflict democratization.

---

33   See Appendix II, based on models from Figure 25.

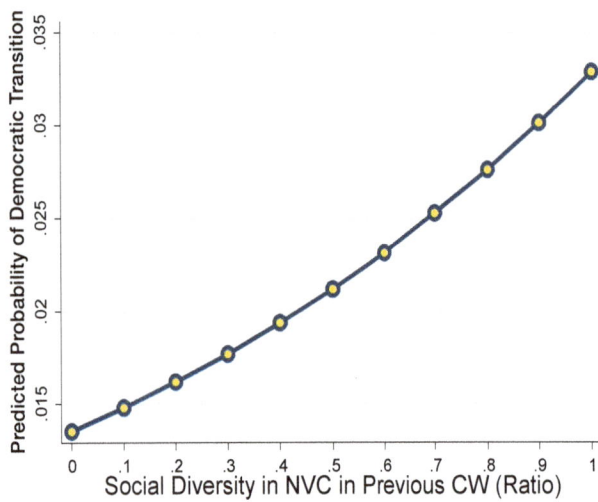

Graph 12a

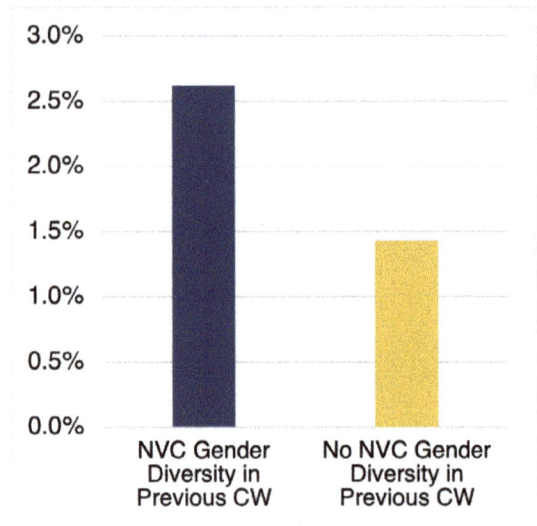

Graph 12b

FIGURE 12. Social Diversity of Wartime Nonviolent Campaigns (NVC),
Women's Participation, and Post-Conflict Democratization, based on data from 1955 to 2010

Social, Organizational, and Gender Diversity of Campaigns and Post-Conflict Democratization

Figure 12 displays predictions from the regression results concerning social and organizational diversity; both are associated with more successful nonviolent campaigns. Figure 12a shows that the social diversity of wartime nonviolent campaigns has important consequences for post-conflict democratization.

As the social diversity of a nonviolent campaign increases, the likelihood of post-conflict democratization exponentially increases. Figure 12b shows that women's participation is an important factor in a campaign's social diversity. Wartime nonviolent campaigns with women's participation nearly doubles the predicted likelihood of post-conflict democratization, compared to campaigns without gender diversity.

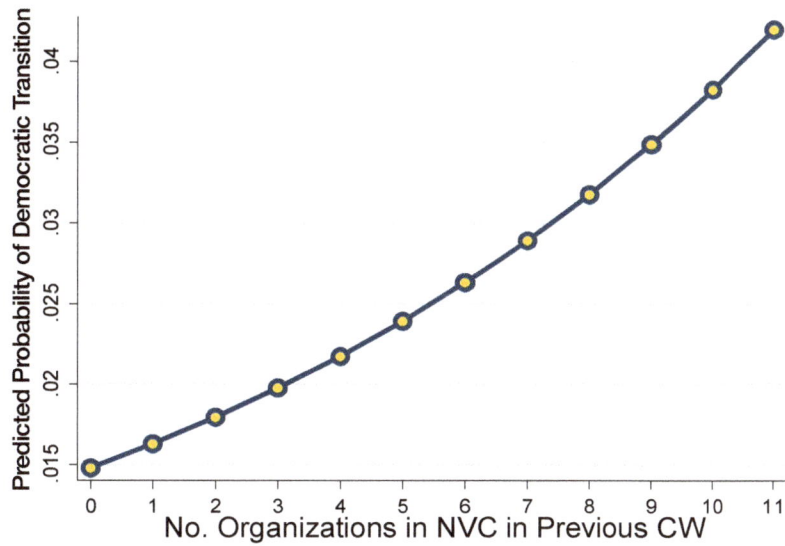

FIGURE 13. Organizational Diversity of Wartime Nonviolent Campaigns (NVC) and Post-Conflict Democratization, based on data from 1955 to 2010

Figure 13 shows that the organizational diversity of nonviolent campaigns also has important consequences for post-conflict democratization. The evidence here suggests that the more organizationally diverse a nonviolent campaign during civil war, the more likely democratization is to occur after the end of civil war.

Organizational diversity (i.e., shared and dispersed power), social diversity (i.e., coalition building), and women's participation (i.e., inclusion)—factors which are often key requirements for successfully mobilizing nonviolent campaigns in the first place (Abbs 2020)—all appear to have important and positive effects on the period after the end of civil war and the power sharing and power transfer thereafter.

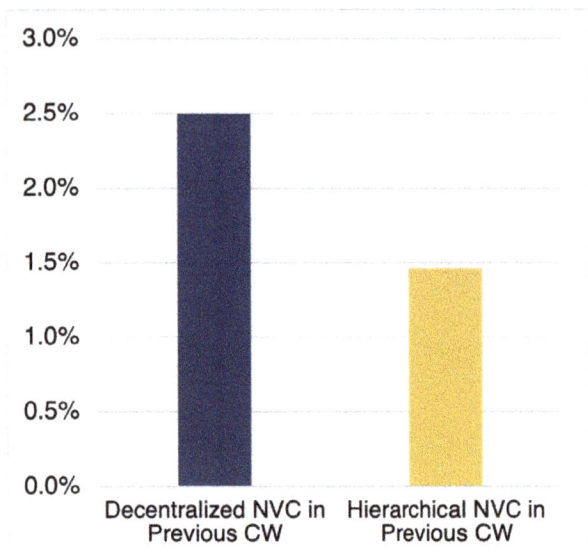

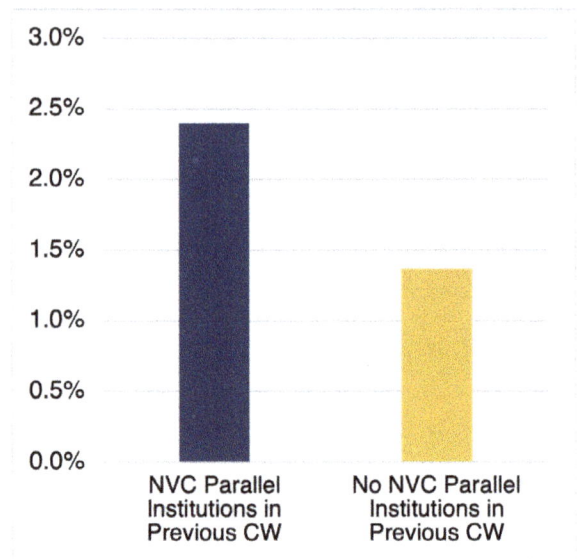

FIGURE 14. Leadership Structure and Parallel Institutions of Wartime Nonviolent Campaigns (NVC) and Post-Conflict Democratization, based on data from 1955 to 2010

Campaign Leadership Structure, Alternative Institutions, and Post-Conflict Democratization

Finally, Figure 14 reports the predicted likelihood of post-conflict democratization given the presence of nonviolent campaigns that have decentralized structures and those with parallel institutions. Decentralized leadership is by its very nature a dispersion of power among different factions and is assumed to make a nonviolent campaign more adaptable. This often coincides with movements that are very socially and organizationally diverse. Graph 14a shows that wartime decentralized nonviolent campaigns also promote a positive pathway for post-conflict democratization; decentralized nonviolent campaigns during civil war are nearly twice as likely to precede post-conflict democratization than hierarchical movements.

Graph 14b shows a similar trend for nonviolent campaigns with parallel institutions. Such institutions are often assumed to be an important basis for future participatory democracy and the prediction from the regression analysis provides evidence for this; democratization after the end of civil war is twice as likely when a wartime nonviolent campaign has parallel institutions, compared to cases where campaign lacks parallel institutions.[34]

---

34   See Appendix II, based on models from Figure 25.

6. Evidence from In-Depth Case Study Analysis

Having found empirical evidence for most of the assumptions (1a, 1c, and 2–8) using large-N data analysis, this chapter offers an in-depth investigation of two cases: South Africa and Mali. These studies explore the campaign-focused mechanisms that were analyzed earlier in the statistical models. We focus here on the impact of nonviolent campaigns during civil war on peace and democratization within specific contexts of these two countries. Overall, these case studies provide further support for the assumptions explored in this monograph.

6.1. South Africa's Democratic Movement (1983–94): The Road to Peace and Democracy

The well-known struggle against apartheid provides an interesting case where sustained nonviolent resistance led to a peace transition of power that would end the conflict and bring about democracy after the civil war ended. This transition was achieved in the face of unprecedented obstacles in a highly industrialized state with a powerful military and a complex, repressive, and racist colonial system of apartheid. This case distinctly highlights the important role of nonviolent resistance in achieving a peaceful and negotiated transition of power.

Background to the Mass Democratic Movement

The apartheid system was a colonial system that went beyond public segregation. Apartheid controlled the movement of people through a policy of "influx control," keeping surplus labor in isolated Bantustans that were created miles from urban and industrialized areas under the 1959 Bantu Self-Government Act (Zunes 1999).

Amid extreme socioeconomic and political inequalities, nonviolent resistance has a long history in South Africa. The First Defiance Campaign (1952–59), led by the African National Congress (ANC), involved various activities of non-cooperation and boycotts against the apartheid regime. The campaign lost momentum and turned into rather ineffective armed resistance after 1960 when police fired into crowds and killed 69 people at Sharpeville. In 1976, protests by school children reignited major nonviolent resistance, drawing support from the Black Consciousness Movement that had emerged following the banning of the ANC. The campaign dissipated after the Soweto Uprising in 1976 that cost the lives of 575 people (Lodge 2011), and by 1977 the Black Consciousness Movement lost its momentum when its national leader, Steve Biko, was killed in police custody.

It was a series of increasingly repressive political reforms between 1982 and 1983 that preceded the emergence of the mass democratic movement. The first reform, the Black Local Authorities Act, aimed to pacify the black population by providing token local political representation. The second reform, a new constitution, created a tricameral legislature consisting of an all-white House of Assembly, plus separate and unequal chambers for Coloured (multiracial) and Asian South Africans. No chamber or political representation was established for Black South Africans.

In response, Oliver Tambo, head of the African National Congress (ANC), called for a "Year of United Action" and a merging of all pro-democratic forces in January 1983 (Lodge 2011). The mass democratic movement that emerged was an extraordinary alliance between the ANC, the newly formed United Democratic Front (UDF), and the Congress of South African Trade Unions (COSATU), representing an incredible array of local organizations and calling for a multiracial democracy, and nonviolent mobilization and resistance to achieve it.

The coalition included civil society organizations, trade unions, students, church groups, and women's groups representing all races and united by the goal of multiracial democracy and an end to exploitation.

The first organization to emerge was the UDF in 1983, which started from a campaign to boycott elections to the newly created local political authorities for Black South Africans, under the Black Local Authorities Act and isolated from the new tricameral national legislature representing non-Blacks. This boycott was aimed at undermining the legitimacy of the new authorities and clearly discriminatory political structure (Lodge 2011). At its inception, the UDF was a coalition of 565 organizations, and it grew to 700 organizations by the late 1980s (Karis 1986). The coalition included civil society organizations, trade unions, students, church groups, and women's groups representing all races and united by the goal of multiracial democracy and an end to exploitation. The UDF was able to coordinate boycotts, strikes, and protests across the country and promoted a range of issues including housing, rent, transportation, and education (Price 1991; Zunes 1999; Schock 2005; Kurtz 2009).

COSATU was formed two years later in 1985, and unified 500,000 workers into one nationwide federation of trade unions. Prior to 1985, unions had been smaller, dispersed, and engaged in conventional activities focused on workers' rights. After the formation of the UDF in 1983, trade unions came under increasing pressure to join the democratic movement. Drawing on the strength of its workplace network and coalition of grassroots organizations, COSATU joined the democratic movement in alliance with UDF and the ANC, but retained its independence (Price 1991; Adler and Webster 2005; Schock 2005). By the end of the 1980s, COSATU boasted a membership of over a million people (Schock 2005).

The ANC had once led nonviolent campaigns in the 1950s, but after the Sharpeville massacre began advocating the violent overthrow of the apartheid regime. Young leaders, including Nelson Mandela, created the armed wing of the ANC, the *uMkhonto we Sizwe* ("Spear of the Nation"), but this had little effect on the regime despite foreign support, extensive training, and the military sabotage of state targets (Schock 2005). Decades later and whilst in prison, Mandela and other ANC leaders re-embraced nonviolent resistance to bring down the apartheid government.

The ANC's long-term goals of securing a transition to a non-racial democratic state were enshrined within the 1954 Freedom Charter. These goals would later be shared by the UDF and COSATU, who would recognize the ANC's senior role in the struggle against apartheid (Lodge 2011). Despite its escalation of armed rebellion in the 1980s, the ANC had a cohesive grassroots network, strong external legitimacy, and a well-established diplomatic network that was used to lobby international actors and highlight the plight of South Africans. Through the 1980s, the ANC began to increasingly realize the growing potential of nonviolent resistance relative to its armed activities (Schock 2005).

Constructive Conflict: Forcing Negotiations by Escalating the Conflict, Not the Violence

The democratic movement had a significant impact on transforming the conflict, eventually forcing negotiations and a peaceful transition to democracy. Central to the strategy and eventual success of the movement was the engagement in constructive conflict, where the movement chose to significantly escalate its strategy of nonviolent economic non-cooperation to destabilize the apartheid system in ways that would undermine the repressive apparatus and force the regime to negotiate a new power arrangement and the end of apartheid.

The UDF's first major campaign, the boycotting of local elections, effectively undermined the legitimacy of the Black Local Authorities Act as well as the new tricameral legislature, as only 1 in 5 Coloureds and 1 in 7 Asians casted their vote after the campaign (Seekings 2000). The UDF then led an unprecedented number of strikes and boycotts. In November 1984, 400,000 students and 800,000 workers engaged in a "stayaway" in the Transvaal province (Price 1991). In 1985, UDF affiliates boycotted white-owned businesses in Port Elizabeth and demanded the removal of soldiers from the townships, the desegregation of public facilities, and an end for workplace discrimination (Ackerman and DuVall 2000). In 1984–85, 390 strikes and boycotts were recorded across the country (Thompson 2001).

The boycotts were so threatening that the regime declared a state of emergency for the first time in 23 years and the formal machinery of local government completely broke down (Thompson 2001; Schock 2005). A new alternative government, or "committees," were set up to run many of the townships, which further undermined the state (Zunes 1999). In March 1986, the movement launched the National Education Crisis Committee, which was funded by the community to provide education as many teachers were fired for ignoring the state curriculum, and health committees were set up by UDF-affiliated health workers (Price 1991).

By 1988, with the emergence of COSATU, support and participation in the campaign had increased to levels that were unsustainable for regime survival, including a three-day general strike in June that involved more than 3 million students and workers and paralyzed industry in an already weakened South African economy (Kurtz 2009).

There were two key reasons why the campaign was successful in transforming destructive conflict into constructive conflict and forcing a peaceful transition. The first reason is the decentralized structure of the democratic movement and its dispersed leadership. This allowed the movement to mitigate state repression and helped to ensure backfire when an increase in state repression encouraged more movement mobilization and attracted international economic sanctions. Seeking international attention and lobbying for international sanctions became another key strategy of the movement using the efforts of activists in the South African diaspora.

The second reason was sustained economic non-cooperation. Since the regime was dependent on non-white labor, this gave the movement leverage against the regime. Eventually this pressure started to draw support from segments of the regime's allies, including reformist elites that were increasingly alienated from the ruling elite, and white businesses feeling the pain of strikes and international sanctions.

Decentralized Structure and Leadership: Building Momentum While Adapting to Repression

A decentralized campaign and dispersed leadership among the UDF, COSATU, ANC, and the multiple organizations within the federations made it adaptable to withstand state repression. By the mid-1980s the UDF-led movement was actively resisting the apartheid regime in every urban center and homeland across the country, stretching the security forces thin and reducing the effectiveness of repression.

The UDF was also galvanized by local initiatives, with the many local civic and student groups within the UDF organizing local boycotts and protests on behalf of the UDF (Lodge 2001). While the state of emergency weakened the national structure of the UDF, the combined effect of local networks of multiple organizations and community-based groups and the dispersed leadership across the country allowed the UDF to adapt and provided the movement with the ability for tactical innovation (Schock 2005).

After the state of emergency was declared, state violence significantly increased within the townships and against protesters and activists (Thompson 2001). While the repression began to take its toll on the UDF—which was eventually banned in 1988— COSATU assumed a leadership role and continued to provide support to grassroots groups affiliated with the

UDF and its allies. Coalition building and cooperation between federated organizations allowed the democratic movement to continue to gain momentum despite increasing state repression (Schock 2005). COSATU was able to increase the pressure on the regime, through a range of union actions, protests, and boycotts that significantly disrupted businesses and the economy, thereby limiting the broader impact of repression and the intended purpose of the state of emergency (Adler and Webster 1995; Seekings 2000).

In the end, the 1985 state of emergency backfired. It failed to subdue the democratic movement, which managed to adapt and increase its domestic mobilization and support. It also played into the external strategy of the movement to garner international support for economic sanctions and provided the international media with footage that highlighted the horrors of apartheid (Price 1991; Guelke 2004).

Redressing Power Asymmetries Through Economic Non-Cooperation

As momentum built, the movement was increasingly able to hurt the regime economically through a strategy of economic non-cooperation. The regime's power was reliant on the obedience of non-white labor that constituted 80 percent of the population. Economic non-cooperation allowed the movement to attack the system that sustained apartheid, thereby redressing power asymmetries between the apartheid regime and anti-apartheid democratic movement that would eventually force peace talks (Zunes 1999; Guelke 2005).

The democratic movement learned from the 1973 strikes in Durban, which had demonstrated the vulnerability of the South African economy due to its reliance on black workers. Economic non-cooperation provided a path for nonviolent resistance to succeed and hurt the apartheid government, in ways that would force the government into negotiations (Zunes 1999). This resistance strategy to undermine the economy was everywhere throughout the 1980s aimed at reducing the power of the regime. Rent boycotts during the state of emergency in 1985 involved half a million households (Seekings 2000). A three-day "stayaway" in June 1988 cost the South African manufacturing sector around 500 million Rand with 70 percent of workers remaining at home. In September, a stayaway in remembrance for the Sharpeville massacre led to almost 100 percent of workers refusing to go to work (Price 1991). Between 1986 and 1990, more workdays were lost to economic non-cooperation than in the previous 75 years (Schock 2005).

Economic non-cooperation was then combined with a broader campaign that aimed to destabilize every aspect of apartheid rule—the 1989 Defiance Campaign. This campaign effectively undermined the regime's ability to enforce apartheid laws, thus altering power asymmetries that maintained the conflict and apartheid regime (Zunes 1999). Illegal multiracial peace marches emerged across the country, and sustained demonstrations essentially neutralized the state of emergency (Smuts and Wescott 1991). Activists renamed public facilities after exiled anti-apartheid leaders. Clergy illegally married interracial couples (Zunes 1999). By the end of the decade, consumer boycotts were taking their toll on white businesses, raising questions about the viability of segregation. Local chambers of commerce and business began to lobby the government to end segregation and withdraw soldiers from townships (Swilling 1988; Schock 2005; Lodge 2011).

By the end of the 1980s, after years of economically damaging unrest, those keen for change were not limited to the anti-apartheid grassroots opposition; members of the white establishment joined the democratic movement, including business leaders, the mayor of Cape Town, and the leaders of the formal opposition Democratic Party (Smuts and Westcott 1991).

Economic non-cooperation, along with international sanctions, brought about in part by the movement's external strategy to gain outside support for economic sanctions and a string of international activities (e.g., the lobbying and activism of Desmond Tutu, who won the Nobel Peace Prize in 1984) shifted support that also altered power asymmetries as it generated divisions among the economic and political elites on the government-side.

Eventually, the movement's increasing ability to hurt the South African economy forced the political elites into concessions (Schock 2005). The "securocrats," a more hardline faction that imposed the state of emergency, were increasingly isolated by the business community and moderate elites calling for reform. By 1989, they were forced out by reformists who wanted to end South Africa's economic isolation. This ended the state of emergency, and the ANC and UDF were legalized. In 1990 came the release of prisoners, including freeing Nelson Mandela, who, by then, was clearly an authoritative and accepted leader of the mass democratic movement even though he neither led nor organized it. Ultimately, liberalization provided the necessary political space for negotiations to begin (Price 1991; Schock 2005).

By this time, defectors were also essentially given a way out—due to the multiracial and nonviolent stance of the democratic movement—through a national reconciliation process. Such a process made prospects of a multiracial democracy less threatening. The UDF and COSATU had both endorsed the ANC's Freedom Charter and called for the unity of all democrats, regardless of religion or race (Thompson 2001). The South African Council of Churches (SACC), led by 1984 Nobel Peace Prize winner Desmond Tutu, gained considerable support from the white population and called on all followers to disobey apartheid laws (Zunes 1999).

While the UDF and other groups often refused to denounce the armed violence of the ANC, they did distance themselves from it. Desmond Tutu consistently challenged anti-apartheid and township violence and Winnie Mandela was ostracized by the movement after she began sanctioning violent activities (Zunes 1999). This helped to lure white popular opinion away from continued racial domination. In March 1992, two-thirds of whites voted 'yes' in a national referendum on whether to negotiate an end to apartheid (Kurtz 1999).

By the early 1990s, the struggle had moved to the negotiation table. The nonviolent resistance movement provided the anti-apartheid block with a strong bargaining position to push through democratic demands and legitimize a process of reconciliation that led to the Truth and Reconciliation Commission (Kurtz 2009). On September 14, 1991, 26 organizations signed the National Peace Accord, which ended the armed conflict between the ANC and the government and set up a transition period that would establish multi-party politics and conflict resolution structures at the local level.

Table 10. Summary of Key Findings: Mass Democratic Movement in South Africa (1983–94)

MECHANISMS OF CHANGE AND OVERALL IMPACT:	
Impact on Peace	The mass democratic movement forced peace negotiations and an end to apartheid using two key strategies: 1. Economic non-cooperation (i.e., mass strikes and boycotts) that exposed and exploited—for the benefit of the movement—the apartheid regime's reliance on black workers. By the late 1980s the apartheid government had little option but to seek negotiations amid a struggling economy and defections from economic and political elites. 2. An external strategy of gaining international support; making state repression backfire and using both domestic and external activists to lobby for international sanctions which were eventually implemented.
Impact on Post-Conflict Democracy	The constructive focus on non-racial campaigning and the building of diverse coalitions had a significant impact on conflict transformation, racial equality, and reconciliation. Central to the mass democratic movement was the adoption of the ANC's Freedom Charter which called for a racially equal participatory democracy in South Africa. This became a blueprint for South Africa's impressive transition, involving 26 organizations and the eventual adoption of the highly liberal and inclusive "rainbow constitution."
IMPACT OF SPECIFIC CAMPAIGN ATTRIBUTES:	
Success and Campaign Size	Without the leverage of economic non-cooperation that undermined the economy, the apartheid government had little incentive to accept peace talks. The size of the strikes and boycotts were critical, involving millions of South African workers and lost working hours. This also gave civil society a strong voice in the conflict.
Social Diversity and Participation of Women	The movement's diversity allowed it to undermine the apartheid government, both economically (with participants from all sectors of the economy) and politically (encouraging different racial groups to boycott elections, undermine apartheid institutions, and defect). Through the United Democratic Movement Women's Organisation, women were important participants and leaders in the movement.
Organizational Diversity and Decentralized Leadership	Coalitions within the movement represented a huge number of organizations and were unified and well organized. This advantage strongly relates to the importance of a decentralized leadership structure, which made the movement adaptable and innovative. When the apartheid government repressed one organization, another took over the leadership role. When national leaders were arrested, local networks carried on unabated. Coalition building also promoted power sharing and democratic principles, central to South Africa's transition to peace.
Alternative Institutions	Many alternative institutions in the movement were localized and had a great deal of autonomy. The non-racial actions of these institutions undermined the apartheid system (e.g., setting up local committees to provide services such as education, health care, legal recourse; the National Education Crisis Committee; illegal marrying of interracial couples).

While the legacy of apartheid still impacts South Africa (e.g., poverty, crime, and social unrest), the legacy of the democratic movement has been a relatively well-functioning democracy that is free from civil war. The specific attributes of a campaign shown to increase the likelihood of peace and democratization in the statistical analysis are clearly evident in South Africa's democratic movement. The size of the mass democratic movement, high levels of social and organizational diversity, decentralized leadership, and alternative institutions all played hugely important roles in ending apartheid and transforming South Africa into a peaceful democracy (see Table 10).

6.2. Mali's March Revolution (1991–96): Democratization and Impact on Peace

Mali in the early 1990s represents an interesting case because the pro-democracy campaign first brought about democratization during the ongoing Tuareg rebellion in 1991, before laying the foundation for a peace process that would lead to an eventual peace agreement with the Tuareg rebels in 1996.

This development represents an alternative causal pathway, where the overthrow of a dictatorship and democratization increased the ripeness for a subsequent resolution of armed rebellion. This is similar to the case of Nepal, where the removal of the monarchy—which had little incentive to seek peace—increased political space that paved the way for the peace process.

Background to Mali's March Revolution

The Republic of Mali gained independence from France in 1960. The first left-wing government was overthrown eight years later in a military coup d'etat. For decades the country remained under a military dictatorship led by General Mousa Traore, who outlawed all opposition political parties. Those close to the regime enriched themselves, but the standard of living in the country plummeted during the 1980s as the regime misused international aid and implemented austerity measures that were advocated by the International Monitory Fund. This laid the foundation for both violent rebellion and nonviolent opposition.

Nonviolent opposition groups began openly challenging the regime and pushed for democracy in October 1990. At the forefront of the nonviolent dissent was the Alliance for Democracy in Mali (ADEMA), who were able to build on growing international pressure for the military regime to democratize (Smith 2001). In 1990, opposition demands for greater political rights were not met and government killings and arrests of opposition leaders continued unabated. The successful mass pro-democracy campaign emerged in March 1991 after talks between the government and the opposition failed. In alliance with the Mali Pupils and Students Association (AEEM) and the National Committee for Democratic Initiative (CNID), ADEMA coordinated and launched mass protests and strikes (or *événements*) throughout the month (Turrittin 1991; Zunes and Nesbitt 2009; Passanante and Rennebohm 2011).

The turning point came at the end of March. On March 22, the movement led a protest march to mark the end of a 48-hour strike. Government forces opened fired and threw grenades into the crowds of protesters, killing 25 people (Turrittin 1991). The outrage led thousands of protesters to return to the streets the next day. On March 23, a further 150 people were killed by government forces. This led to a joint declaration from opposition groups demanding Traore's resignation, the implementation of an interim government, and multi-party elections. On March 25, thousands of workers took part in a general strike and joined the pro-democracy rally, followed by the resignation of General Djibril Diallo and mass military defections, as soldiers also joined the protests. On March 26, Lieutenant Colonel Touré was arrested by the head of the presidential guard, Amadou Touré. Promising to respect opposition demands, Touré set up a joint military-civilian interim government in preparation for multi-party elections (Passanante and Rennebohm 2011).

The Tuareg armed rebellion emerged a year prior to the pro-democracy campaign in June 1990. The Tuareg people are a nomadic population that can be found across the northern desert region of Mali—as well as in Niger, Libya, and Algeria—in territory referred to as Azawad. Resentments over government policies and political inequalities posed persistent questions about self-determination and increased autonomy. This tension was exacerbated by the misuse of international aid meant for droughts that impacted the north between 1972 and 1974 and in 1985, the brutal repression of dissent in 1985 and 1989, and communal violence (Turrittin 1991).

Across the border in Libya, exiled Tuareg received military training but were expelled from the country after economic decline in the 1980s. This moved a large number of well trained and well-equipped fighters back south to Mali. Recruiting largely from these returning exiles and citing historic grievances, the Popular Movement for the Liberation of Azawad (MPLA) marked the start of the Tuareg rebellion in June 1990, with an attack on a garrison in Menaka. This triggered widespread violence and a brutal military crackdown (UCDP Encyclopedia 2019).

The March Revolution that occurred during this armed conflict had a concerted impact on the peace process; the movement was able to redress power asymmetries between the regime and opposition forces by removing the repressive military government through a nonviolent campaign built on coalition building and shared power between participating factions. This wartime democratic transition widened political space and allowed for constructive and inclusive engagement with Tuareg opposition in the north.

Redressing Power Asymmetries Through Coalition Building and Decentralized Leadership

Like most civil wars, the Tuareg rebellion can be defined as an asymmetric relationship between a strong military government and weaker rebels. Initially, there were few obvious incentives for the stronger military regime to seek a peaceful settlement of the conflict. Moreover, the army responded harshly to the rebellion, summarized in the words of one parachute commander that "the solution concerning the Tuaregs is their extermination. I have come here to take care of that" (New Humanitarian 2012). Despite the hardline approach, initial peace negotiations took place in late 1990 and the Tamanrasset peace agreement was signed in January 1991, resulting in a ceasefire and the release of prisoners.[35]

The pro-democracy movement that led to the March Revolution in 1991 altered power asymmetries in two key ways. First, the Tamanrasset peace negotiations in late 1990 were forced by the need to divert troops back to the capital amid the emerging nonviolent unrest in December and rising international pressure (UCDP Encyclopedia 2019). Second, the movement forced the military ruler President Traoré to step down, opening up political space. The revolution had two consequences: it reduced the power of the military in Mali, placing more power into the hands of civil society that had used nonviolent resistance to force change, and it paved the way for an inclusive multi-party democracy. Both were crucial for reigniting the peace process, offering the Tuaregs political representation and devolved powers in the new political system, and ultimately leading to a peace agreement with the Tuareg rebels in 1996.

The pro-democracy movement led by ADEMA had a strategy of using mass protest and persuasion (mass pro-democracy demonstrations) and occasional non-cooperation (through general strikes by union workers and students) to quickly remove the military dictatorship and introduce a multi-party system. ADEMA organized a series of mass demonstrations in collaboration with the National Committee for Democratic Initiative (CNID) and the Mali Pupils and Students Association (AEEM). These groups were keen to make government repression backfire, using public outrage about state violence to gain increased support for the movement. Honoring the deaths of previous pro-democracy activists, on March 17, 1991, all three groups organized the "National Day of Martyrs" demonstration, bringing 100,000 people into the capital's streets.

Women also played an important role in the campaign, with more than 2,000 women participating in demonstrations and attempting to mitigate violence against protesters. On March 23, the death of five female protesters created even more outrage and encouraged more people to join the protests (Passanante and Rennebohm 2011). Two days later, the National Union of Workers organized a mass strike, adding economic non-cooperation to the movement's repertoire of tactics.

While the pro-democracy campaign did not table demands for peace talks, the nonviolent activities did lead to a change in regime during the armed conflict, which revitalized the peace

---

35   The accord also provided a provision for regional autonomy in the north, leading the MPLA to reduces its demands from independence to autonomy and to drop "Liberation" from its name. However, the agreement was marked by mistrust and led to splits within the rebels, as hardliners maintained their claim for independence. The agreement was never implemented as the military regime was removed from power two months later in the March Revolution.

process. Similar to the case of South Africa, the pro-democracy movement had a decentralized leadership and the exceptional ability to cooperate and build coalitions, which were both key to its success, making the movement adaptable to repression and bringing together various social groups.

ADEMA developed its decentralized organizational structure and social base during the military rule when political parties were illegal. The group formed as a coalition of various political parties that were opposed to the regime and operated covertly. Prior to the March Revolution, ADEMA quickly broadened its coalition with trade unions and student groups, working with broad sectors of the population to initiate mass demands for democracy. Leadership was not only dispersed throughout ADEMA but also across the various organizations within the pro-democracy movement. The movement was therefore adaptable to state violence and able to build momentum despite mass arrests of its leaders (Nepstad 2011).

The pro-democracy movement led by ADEMA had a strategy of using mass protest and persuasion and occasional non-cooperation to quickly remove the military dictatorship and introduce a multi-party system.

During the campaign, the movement not only included a consortium of organizations but also actively encouraged broad participation from civil society, including poor and wealthy urban citizens, persons with disabilities, and women both young and old—making the movement resilient to repression (Turrittin 1991). This coalition building had a distinct legacy, as the movement continued to reach out and form alliances with other stakeholders during the democratic transition—including stakeholders from the Tuareg region—allowing the movement to maintain its influence and legitimacy, and promoting ideas of consensus-seeking and power sharing (Zunes and Nesbitt 2009; Zunes 2012).

The most important attribute of the movement was its geographical influence. This largely relates to ADEMA, which had the support of teachers and health professionals who were able to spread its democratic and consensus-seeking message to rural communities throughout the country. This helped to expand ADEMA's network, support base, and legitimacy to almost all areas of Mali, including the north (Zunes and Nesbitt 2009; Vengroff 1993). As the statistical analysis shows, greater social diversity within a campaign is important in aiding the transformation of civil war. Here the regional diversity of the movement and its ability to reach rural communities were particularly important.[36]

---

36 Figure 23 in Appendix II shows that regional diversity within a movement is strongly associated with the likelihood of a negotiated agreement.

The movement also encompassed students, trade unionists, and others, supported by traditional singing storytellers that helped spread the movement's message throughout the country (Zunes and Nesbitt 2009; Zunes 2012). Social diversity and coalition building enabled the entire movement to keep the pressure on the government and gave a voice to various areas of the country, effectively changing the balance of power within Mali. Moreover, the movement's development of a nationwide network provided vital lessons for democratization, tackling the root causes of the Tuareg conflict.

Legacy of the March Revolution: Opening Up Political Space in the Transition Period

After overthrowing the military dictatorship, civilian leaders from the pro-democracy campaign formed the transitional government with reformist army officers. The transition government immediately brought all parties into the democratization process ahead of the multi-party elections in 1992. Between July and August 1991, the transitional government set up a national conference in the capital, inviting a range of stakeholders and members of civil society to discuss the establishment of democracy in Mali. The national conference invited 2,000 individuals representing a broad range of civil society, who participated in reimagining the political system and created the Third Republic (Wing 2013). The conference led to a new constitution introducing multi-party elections within a semi-presidential and proportionally representative electoral system, designed to be inclusive and to accommodate the diversity of interests across Mali. This opened up political space, leading to the creation of 47 political parties (roughly five main parties and a serious of regional parties), including parties from the northern Tuareg regions (Vengroff 1993).

The ADEMA-led transitional government also signed various pacts with key movements, including workers unions (*Pacte social*), and student groups (*Memorandum de l'AEEM*) (Vengroff and Kone 1995). As part of this process, the transitional government sought talks with the Tuareg rebels and signed the *Pact du nord* soon after Mali's first multiparty elections on April 11, 1992 (Ibid.). The settlement marked the formal start of a new, more conciliatory peace process between the democratic government and the rebels, with the pact seeking a "peaceful, negotiated, just and final solution to the painful armed conflict" (United Nations 1992). The Nord Pact specifically focused on redefining the relationship between the north and south of Mali, including provisions for demilitarization, integration of rebels into the Malian army, an ambitious economic development project, and greater regional autonomy through the creation of local assemblies (Chauzal and van Damme 2015).

Legacy of the Campaign: Constructive Attempts of Violence Mitigation and Inclusive Solutions

In 1992, the new ADEMA-led democratic government aimed to resolve the Tuareg conflict through inclusive and conciliatory mechanisms. This first consisted of creating an accountability mechanism that encouraged local dialogues and conciliation and that documented human rights abuses.

Annual forums known as the Question and Answer Assembly (or *Espace d'interpellation démocratique,* EID), were created to find solutions to localized issues, including in the north. This was combined with an ambitious economic development program, supported by national and regional dialogues to discuss healthcare, education, and the judicial and electoral reforms at a time when illiteracy rates in Mali exceeded 70 percent (Wing 2013).

An important component of the EID forums was a mechanism to monitor human rights violations, aimed at increasing accountability and mitigating violence. Many of the grievances in the north related to extreme repression that was carried out by the military. This mechanism allowed Mali citizens to report human rights violations directly to government officials, while judicial concerns and court cases were broadcasted on radio and television (Wing 2013). The president of the new democratic government and ADEMA leader, Alpha Oumar Konaré, twice commuted death sentences for the former President Traore, to promote the new democratic government's conciliatory approach (Smith 2001).

A second constructive approach to solving the Tuareg conflict is related to ADEMA's political strategy of decentralizing political power to local assemblies. The strategy promoted a process of national unity in exchange for demands of local self-government (Kirby and Murray 2010). The introduction of the 1992 constitution and rapid decentralization were concerted efforts to consolidate democracy across Mali, stimulating more responsive and legitimate democratic institutions, while at the same time providing meaningful political representation for the Tuaregs—aimed at defusing the Tuareg rebellion by institutionalizing regional autonomy as agreed in the peace talks (Smith 2001; Saraceno 2015).

The boundaries for the new devolved local communes were not imposed, but instead were negotiated through dialogue with neighboring villages. Regional forums gave civil society a role in local education, health programs, and infrastructure projects (Wing 2013). In 1994, amid increasing violence in the north (mostly between Tuareg factions), the government set up regional "concertations" across the country (or *Concertations regionals*). These "concertations facilitated inter-community dialogue so that people could address concerns and engage in open political discussions (Lode 2002; Wing 2013). The ADEMA government resisted pressure to arm local and ethnic pro-government self-defense militia in the north, focusing instead on finding solutions to the violence through dialogue and consensus (Lode 2002).

The peacebuilding efforts of the democratic government, brought about by the March Revolution, eventually bore fruit in 1996 when a fully comprehensive peace agreement was signed by all factions. The case of Mali largely reflects the key findings of the statistical analysis and bears similarities to what occurred in Nepal in 2005—the impact of nonviolent revolution (in short- to medium-term) on peace and democratization was largely positive (see Table 11 for a summary of these findings).

Table 11. Summary of Key Findings: ADEMA and March Revolution in Mali (1991–1996)

MECHANISMS OF CHANGE AND OVERALL IMPACT:	
Impact on Democracy During the Civil War	In Mali, democracy came before a negotiated civil war settlement, brought about by the ADEMA-led March Revolution, using a strategy of persuasion (i.e., mass protest) to remove the military dictator. The ADEMA-led transitional government was quick to bring all parties into the political process ahead of elections in 1992—47 political parties, including Tuareg parties. This empowered civil society and opened up necessary political space for the peace process with the Tuareg rebels.
Impact on Peace (After Democracy was Achieved)	The new ADEMA-led government continued the constructive approach of the March Revolution into the post-transition era, engaging in coalition building and power sharing. The transitional government first signed various pacts with workers unions (*Pacte social*), student groups (*Memorandum de l'AEEM*) and the Tuareg rebels to initiate the peace process (*Pact du nord*). ADEMA's key strategy was to decentralize political power to simultaneously entrench democracy while satisfying Tuareg demands for regional autonomy. The ADEMA government continued to empower civil society by creating Question and Answer Assemblies (EID), using civil society actors to find solutions to localized issues, create regional concertations to facilitate inter-community dialogue, and document human rights abuses to improve accountability. In 1996, this led to a comprehensive peace agreement signed by all factions.
IMPACT OF SPECIFIC CAMPAIGN ATTRIBUTES:	
Success and Campaign Size	At its peak the nonviolent movement encouraged 100,000 people into the capital's streets in a city of less than 800,000 people, quickly leading to regime change. This ADEMA-led transition to democracy was critical in opening up the space for a meaningful peace process with the Tuareg rebels.
Social Diversity and Participation of Women	Social diversity was central to the success of the nonviolent movement and had important legacies for the subsequent peace process. ADEMA developed a nationwide network, using teachers and health professionals to spread the message to rural communities. Women's participation was encouraged but was unfortunately far more limited than in South Africa.
Organizational Diversity and Decentralized Leadership	Coalition building and shared leadership were important in bringing about regime change, making the movement adaptable to state repression. This experience of coalition building (i.e., between ADEMA, student groups, and trade unions) continued after the democratic transition, with ADEMA reaching out to stakeholders, Tuareg civil society actors, and the Tuareg rebels.
Alternative Institutions	Alternative institutions played less of a role in Mali than in South Africa. However, the movement created its own parallel media to spread its message. After the revolution, ADEMA successfully transformed into a political party, continuing its strategy of constructive change.

The process of conflict transformation was not perfect in Mali. The 1996 peace agreement with the Tuareg rebels came four years after the 1992 *Pact du nord*, a period in which 6,000 to 8,000 people lost their lives. Moreover, the long-term trajectory of the country has proved more difficult. While political decentralization and democratization have contributed to the stability of Mali for almost two decades, conflict did reoccur briefly in 2006 and again in March 2012, leading to a military coup that overthrew the democratic government. Ultimately, political decentralization aimed at fostering peace, as well as other peace initiatives explored above, were undermined by a lack of funding in one of the world's poorest countries (Chauzal and van Damme 2015; Saraceno 2015). A lack of resources led to a slow implementation of these initiatives that undermined attempts to reinforce democracy and transform the Tuareg conflict in Mali. For instance, the transfer of powers over health, education, and water to local communes only began in 2010 (Wing 2013). Nevertheless, what happened in the country twenty years later cannot be blamed on the 1991 revolution, as other factors and conditions could have independently become pronounced during such a long time.

There is certainly no indication that the pro-democracy movement in 1991 contributed to conflict recurrence in 2006 and 2012 or the military coup in 2012. In the end, matters outside Mali had a huge impact on the country: the Libya conflict in 2011 led to the recruitment, arming, and funding of many Tuareg fighters who would later return to Mali and rekindle armed rebellion in 2012. While it is impossible to know if events would have been different had a nonviolent campaign not emerged, it is clear democratization would have been less likely absent the nonviolent resistance campaign. In turn, without the kind of democracy that emerged in Mali after 1991, it is unlikely the peace process would have been as ambitious or inclusive. Unlike the short-term nature of previous failed agreements and despite Mali's vulnerability, the 1996 peace agreement held for a decade.

7. Key Takeaways of the Monograph

This monograph has provided credence to a positive relationship between largescale nonviolent campaigns, the transformation of civil war, and post-conflict democratization. The main added-value of this study to the existing knowledge about the impact of nonviolent campaigns and movements is its focus on the civil war context—a very difficult environment for any resistance, including a nonviolent one, to operate in. Yet, as it was demonstrated, the findings provide strong evidence that nonviolent resistance can aid the resolution of armed conflict and have a positive impact on post-conflict democratization. Evidence also points to the predictive power of the monograph analysis, since the explored outcomes are consistently more likely to have occurred in cases in which largescale nonviolent movements were active, when compared to cases where these movements were absent. The findings were subsequently reinforced by evidence from South Africa and Mali, which offer further evidence on the positive and complex interplay between nonviolent resistance, civil war, peace, and democratization.

To the best of the author's knowledge, this is the first study to explore this multifaceted relationship in a systematic way, using both statistical and case study approaches. This monograph also represents the first attempt to assess the impact of nonviolent resistance on both the post-conflict phase and post-conflict democratization. This builds on emerging case research that has begun to explore these relationships, but which focuses solely on positive cases where nonviolent resistance has led to peaceful outcomes, such as in Nepal or Liberia. This monograph instead analyzes a large-N dataset, exploring different outcomes across various civil wars globally between 1955 and 2013.

It is important to note, however, that nonviolent campaigns do not always deliver the desired outcomes. Mobilizing nonviolent campaigns is extremely challenging, which makes the cases of South Africa and Mali (among others) all the more remarkable. Mobilizing nonviolent campaigns involves overcoming the apathy and fear of millions of people, developing complex social networks, building coalitions with multiple organizations in often socially divided contexts, sustaining momentum, and fostering tactical innovation. It also requires both material and non-material resources, including creativity, passion, and sacrifices from the activists that participate in nonviolent action. Moreover, these processes have to take place in the context of often acute state repression, where people are at continuous risk of violence—all of which is exacerbated in civil war environments. Nevertheless, as the cases of Mali and South Africa show, nonviolent campaigns have proven far more successful than armed resistance in fostering transitions to peace, despite emerging in contexts that are unfavorable to nonviolent resistance.

Table 12. Key Lessons for Academics, Activists, and Policymakers

ACADEMICS	ACTIVISTS	POLICYMAKERS

(1) Wartime nonviolent campaigns increase the likelihood of civil war negotiated settlements.
 	
(2) Wartime nonviolent campaigns increase the likelihood of post-conflict democratization.
 	
(3) Certain campaign features explain the above positive trends:
 	
  (i) large and more socially diverse participation
 	
  (ii) decentralized leadership structures
 	
  (iii) deployment of alternative institutions
	(1) Peace and democratization can be achieved through nonviolent campaigns.
	
	(2) Activists should learn from the lessons and mistakes of previous wartime campaigns.
	
	(3) Social inclusion, gender diversity, and reaching out to pro-regime segments are critical for transforming violent conflict.
	
	(4) Shared and dispersed leadership is most resilient to state repression and provides a blueprint for post-conflict democracy and power sharing.
	
	(5) The creation of alternative institutions undermines the legitimacy of the state and are preparatory for a future inclusive and participatory democracy.
		(1) Findings in this study debunk misconceptions that nonviolent movements may exacerbate violent conflict.
		
		(2) While caution is always required, external assistance to nonviolent movements (e.g., in the form of monetary support, technical support, negotiation training, sanctions against the regime) represent a positive alternative to military solutions.
		
		(3) Nonviolent activists can support peacebuilding and democratization efforts and should be included and supported in peace initiatives, negotiations, and diplomatic activities.

While these findings show an overall positive trend between nonviolent resistance and civil war outcomes, not all cases have been successful. For instance, in Myanmar, the 8888 Movement in 1988 failed to drive a regime change or end the various ongoing wars in the country. Likewise, the Northern Ireland Civil Rights Association did not have its desired effect on the Troubles in Northern Ireland. While the People Power Movement in the Philippines successfully overthrew Ferdinand Marcos, it had no impact on the Communist armed rebellion in the country.

In the same light, while these findings are based on historical incidents, this may not be representative of future cases, as context plays an important role and must be understood in addition to these findings. For instance, the 2019 Sudanese Revolution, which represents a stunning success of nonviolent movement in a highly repressive and unfavorable setting (Zunes 2021), has already had a positive impact on the conflicts in Darfur and South Kordofan, with the Sudan Revolutionary Front (SRF)—a coalition of rebel groups from Darfur and South Kordofan—signing a peace agreement in August 2020. However, it remains to be seen if the

Sudanese Revolution will have a concerted impact on peace in the region and bring about a fledgling and stable democracy that is more conducive to sustainable peace.

The findings from this study do, however, provide lessons and guidelines that contribute to the growing knowledge in academic scholarship, activists' thinking and strategizing, and approaches to policymaking. The specific contributions and implications of this study for the relevant audiences are highlighted below.

7.1. Contributions and Implications for Academic Scholarship and for the Work of Activists, Practitioners, and Policymakers

Takeaways for Academics

This monograph provides several findings that are relevant to various academic avenues and which have previously been poorly understood in existing academic literature. First, wartime nonviolent campaigns significantly increase the likelihood of peace agreements. As detailed in the case analyses, nonviolent campaigns can pressure governments into seeking negotiations and can foster democratization during civil war. Both, in turn, can contribute to immediate and long-term positive effects on the transformation of armed conflict. This study, however, finds no evidence that nonviolent campaigns in civil war reduce the likelihood of civil war recurrence. Countries with a recent history of civil war remain inherently susceptible to conflict reoccurring at a later point.

Second, the empirical results find a positive relationship between wartime nonviolent resistance and democratization in the post-conflict phase. Many movements promote democratic and inclusive principles, often through creating diverse coalitions that lay the foundation for future power sharing and multi-party politics.

Finally, the attributes of nonviolent campaigns also help explain these positive trends, as demonstrated by case evidence and the empirical findings. Campaigns that successfully achieve their political goals, that mobilize larger numbers of participants, and embrace social and organizational diversity appear to play a crucial role in readdressing power asymmetries by providing movements with the means to hurt a regime. Lessons learned from coalition building can foster desirable impacts on peace and political transition by providing a voice to the wider civil society and increase their say on the design of post-conflict institutions. A decentralized leadership structure also appears to be important in contributing to tactical innovation, in movement's adaptation to harsh government repression, and in maintaining mobilization momentum. Alternative institutions also aid wartime nonviolent resistance in further undermining the legitimacy of the regime and provide a blueprint for future institutions that are developed during a peace process or during democratic transitions.

This monograph has provided many general findings from an exploratory analysis of the impact nonviolent resistance on the transformation of civil war. Yet, many questions remain in what is still an emerging area of scholarship. It is hoped that this monograph will inspire research into a number of important streams of research:

1. Future research needs to look more closely at the causal mechanisms that explain why nonviolent resistance aids the transformation of civil war. In particular, research is needed on less well-known cases beyond the common examples of Nepal, the First Palestinian Intifada, and South Africa. Further, this research should explore cases where nonviolent movements fail to bring about peaceful transitions, as in Myanmar's 8888 Uprising.

2. Much more research is required to explore the impact of nonviolent resistance on post-conflict democratization. Why is post-conflict democracy more durable in some cases but not in others?

3. Further research on the positive relationship between nonviolent resistance and its impact on reducing the chances for civil war recurrence is also needed, as this remains poorly understood. While this monograph finds no evidence of this relationship, this is only exploratory. Under what contexts does nonviolent resistance subsequently reduce the likelihood of civil war relapse?

4. While this monograph highlights the overall impact of nonviolent campaigns, more research is needed to understand the specific influence of different types of nonviolent tactics deployed by civil society organizations: from methods of protest to economic and political non-cooperation, to more institutionalized means of political engagement, lobbying, and negotiations that are often undertaken by these groups during civil war.

5. Beyond anti-government nonviolent campaigns, there is a diverse range of civil society actors using nonviolent action to influence the trajectory of civil war, for example, peace movements—a term that encompasses a huge range of local and national nonviolent actors that are active in many parts of the world and which use a diverse array of nonviolent tactics. We know little about the impact these groups have on civil war and processes of conflict transformation.

Takeaways for Activists

The findings provide a number of takeaway points for activists. First, the findings are a clear indication that nonviolent resistance can have a concerted and positive impact on ending civil war and democratization (both during and after armed conflict). More specifically, this study calls on activists to think carefully and strategize about the mechanisms by which successful long-term outcomes are achieved and to learn lessons from the mistakes and successes of past cases. Coalition building—in recruiting social groups across society, encouraging gender inclusion and involvement by women's groups, and reaching out to pro-regime segments of the population—appears to be crucial in forcing meaningful change and transforming destructive conflict into constructive conflict. Social diversity also promotes innovation that undergirds adaptability, creativity, and inclusive solutions that are crucial for transitions away from destructive and toward constructive conflict and supporting local solutions to the root causes underpinning armed violence.

Maintaining a nonviolent stance and consistently advocating inclusive ideas about the future, while continuing to build a diverse movement, can aid the development of an inclusive societal and political future and reduce fears and uncertainty about this change. It also encourages loyalty shifts in favor of the movement within the pro-regime segment of the population. After any civil war, society fares much better when former enemies can reconcile and learn to live together.

In most contexts, a dispersed leadership and organizational structure appear to be most resilient to violence and less susceptive to a loss of momentum when national leadership of a movement is targeted. Decentralized campaigns encourage local ownership and can draw on the strengths of grassroot initiatives which provide flexibility and tactical innovation that, in turn, reduce the risk of violence for participating activists. Nonviolent resistance movements, regime change, negotiated settlements to civil war, and democratization all seem to go hand-in-hand. Success in one outcome allows success in other outcomes, although it is important to note that maintaining momentum is crucial, of which decentralized campaigns appear to be more successful in achieving. Moreover, dispersed leadership promotes democratic principles of inclusivity, shared responsibility, and decentralized power, which often provide a blueprint for the design of post-conflict democratic institutions.

As the statistical findings and the case of South Africa show, alternative institutions can also play an important role in transforming civil war. Essentially, they can serve two purposes. First, they jointly promote self-governance, autonomy, and inclusive practices, while undermining the legitimacy of unfair and non-inclusive state institutions through creating a situation of dual powers. The Alexandra Action Committee in South Africa represents an excellent example, set up as a de facto government in the Alexandra township near Johannesburg. The Committee drafted a local constitution based on participatory democracy, which devolved powers to a multi-tier system of street committees, block committees (up to 25 houses), and yard committees (four to five houses). The committee led rent strikes, provided service provisions, and formed people's courts, bypassing unjust apartheid institutions (Zunes 1999). Second, alternative institutions generate blueprints for power sharing and participatory democracy, provide solutions to the root causes of conflict, and empower civil society groups to have a say in future political practices. In other cases, alternative institutions come in the form of parallel media, which is vital in spreading the message of a movement and becoming a forum for constructive solutions to conflict.

Takeaways for Policymakers

A common concern for international organizations, peacebuilding NGOs, and state representatives and their agencies is that nonviolent resistance might exacerbate conflict and violence. However, this monograph debunks this misconception with findings that overwhelmingly show the positive impact of nonviolent resistance movements on reducing violence. While policymakers need to be cautious, as the findings of the study show, they should not shy away from helping nonviolent movements. External assistance in the form of monetary and non-monetary aid to resisters and sanctions on the regime were crucial in helping the democratic movement to sustain itself in South Africa. External governments are far too often and too quick to offer financial and material support to armed opposition groups with tragic costs for the warring society (as evidenced by the civil war in Syria). This happens despite the fact that nonviolent movements are both more effective and less detrimental to the long-term peaceful transformation of a country plagued by civil war.

Policymakers can play a more indirect role in pressuring and sanctioning the regime as a way to encourage its moderation and openness to negotiations with peaceful movements.

Yet, any external support for nonviolent movements should be carefully planned as not to generate divisions within a movement or create even greater irreconcilable distance between the power elites and the movement. Policymakers can play a more indirect role in pressuring and sanctioning the regime as a way to encourage its moderation and openness to negotiations with peaceful movements. For instance, economic sanctions played directly into the hands of South Africa's democratic movement in the 1980s, coinciding with the domestic strategy of economic non-cooperation, and encouraged power elites to enter into negotiations with the movement. The international community's embrace of the nonviolent resistance against apartheid, illustrated vividly by the Nobel Peace Prize that was given to Archbishop Desmond Tutu in the midst of the struggle (1994), bestowed further international and moral legitimacy on the movement, reassuring its members that they were on the right side of history and had the support of the free world. Likewise, international pressure on the Mali regime to democratize in 1990 aided the emergence and momentum of the movement there.

A body of research finds that external support can greatly improve outcomes when supporting nonviolent campaigns, particularly in the area of activists' education and training (Chenoweth and Stephan 2021). NGOs can provide key support such as training, knowledge and skills sharing, and capacity building, and can facilitate dialogue between the regime, other armed actors, and nonviolent activists. NGOs can also involve nonviolent movements in the peace process, building on the past experience of countries such as Liberia, Sierra Leone, Guatemala, and Kosovo where civil society was incredibly effective in mitigating violence, directly lobbying peace talks, and pushing for win-win and innovative solutions.

Support can also be provided in the form of connecting active movements to veterans of nonviolent struggles from other countries, circulating manuals, and providing training in negotiation. Activists should pay equal attention into how to transform nonviolent campaigns into roundtable talks and negotiation settlements with the government or the rebels. They should be able to turn from successful activists to skillful negotiators and policymakers. In Mali, ADEMA was very successful developing an effective negotiation capability and transitioning into a political party. In Nepal, the Seven Party Alliance successfully negotiated an agreement with the rebels to join the nonviolent campaign, which subsequently became the blueprint for the peace agreement and power sharing. Wanis-St. John and Rosen's USIP report (2017) examines the role of negotiation within ongoing nonviolent campaigns and concludes that nonviolent resistance and negotiation in civil war are deeply entwined. It is, however, important that international support does not undermine movement autonomy, grassroot initiatives, and the local knowledge of activists, which play to the strengths of nonviolent movements.

As civil war continues to impact the lives of millions of people across the world, it is hoped that this study can significantly enrich the discussion about positive contributions of nonviolent activists in some of the world's most dangerous warzones. In highlighting the role that nonviolent resistance can play in fostering peace settlements and political transitions, it is hoped that civilians are not seen as mere victims but rather important agents of positive political change.

Bibliography

Abbs, Luke. "The Hunger Games: Food Prices, Ethnic Cleavages and Nonviolent Unrest in Africa." *Journal of Peace Research* 57, no. 2 (2020): 281–296.

Abbs, Luke, and Kristian S. Gleditsch. *Ticked Off but Scared Off? Riots and the Fate of Nonviolent Campaigns.* Unpublished Manuscript. Colchester, England: University of Essex, 2019.

Ackerman, Peter, and Jack DuVall. *A Force More Powerful: A Century of Nonviolent Conflict.* New York, NY: Palgrave, 2000.

Adler, Glenn, and Edward Webster. "Challenging Transition Theory: The Labor Movement, Radical Reform, and Transition to Democracy in South Africa." *Politics Society* 23, no. 1 (1995): 75–106.

Arjona, Ana. "Civilian Resistance to Rebel Governance." In *Rebel Governance in Civil War*, edited by Ana Arjona, Nelson Kasfir and Zachariah Mampilly, 180–202. Cambridge, England: Cambridge University Press, 2015.

Barter, Shane. *Civilian Strategy in Civil War: Insights from Indonesia, Thailand, and the Philippines.* New York, NY: Palgrave Macmillan, 2014.

Bartkowski, Maciej. "Alternative Institution Building as Civil Resistance." *Minds of the Movement*, June 13, 2018, **https://www.nonviolent-conflict.org/blog_post/alternative-institution-building-civil-resistance/**.

Bayer, Markus, Felix Bethke, and Daniel Lambach. "The Democratic Dividend of Nonviolent Resistance." *Journal of Peace Research 53,* no. 6 (2016): 758–771.

Bell, Christine, and Sanja Badanjak. "Introducing PA-X: A new peace agreement database and dataset." *Journal of Peace Research* 56, no. 3 (2019): 452–466.

Bell, Christine, and Catherine O'Rourke. "The People's Peace? Peace Agreements, Civil Society, and Participatory Democracy." *International Political Science Review* 28, no. 3 (2007): 293–324.

Bethke, Felix, and Jonathan Pinckney. "Nonviolent Resistance and the Quality of Democracy." *Conflict Management and Peace Science* (Forthcoming).

Bloch, Nadine, and Lisa Schirch. *SNAP: Synergizing Nonviolent Action and Peacebuilding An Action Guide.* Washington, DC: USIP, 2019. **https://www.usip.org/publications/2019/04/snap-synergizing-nonviolent-action-and-peacebuilding**.

Bogati, Subindra, and Ches Thurber. *From the Hills to the Streets to the Table: Civil Resistance and Peacebuilding in Nepal.* Washington, DC: ICNC Press, 2021. **https://www.nonviolent-conflict.org/resource/from-the-hills-to-the-streets-to-the-table-rl/**

Butcher, Charles, John L. Gray, and Liesel Mitchell. "Striking it Free? Organized Labor and the Outcomes of Civil Resistance." *Journal of Global Security Studies* 3, no. 3 (2018): 302–321,

Butcher, Charles, and Isak Svensson. "Manufacturing Dissent: Modernization and the Onset of Major Nonviolent Resistance Campaigns." *Journal of Conflict Resolution* 60, no. 2 (2016): 311–339.

Celestino, Mauricio R., and Kristian S. Gleditsch. "Fresh Carnations or all Thorn, no Rose? Nonviolent Campaigns and Transitions in Autocracies." *Journal of Peace Research* 50, no. 3 (2013): 385–400.

Chauzal, Grégory, and Thibault Van Damme. (2015). *The Roots of Mali's Conflict: Moving Beyond the 2012 Crisis.* The Hague, Netherlands: Clingendael, 2015. **https://www.clingendael. org/sites/default/files/pdfs/The_roots_of_ Malis_conflict.pdf**.

Chenoweth, Erica. *Women's Participation and the Fate of Nonviolent Campaigns: A Report on the Women in Resistance (WiRe) Data Set.* Broomfield, Colorado: One Earth Future Foundation, 2019. **https://dx.doi.org/10.18289/ OEF.2019.041**.

Chenoweth, Erica, and Kathleen Gallagher Cunningham. "Understanding Nonviolent Resistance: An Introduction." *Journal of Peace Research* 50, no. 3 (2013): 271–276.

Chenoweth, Erica, and Orion A. Lewis. "Unpacking Nonviolent Campaigns: Introducing the NAVCO 2.0 Dataset." *Journal of Peace Research* 50, no. 3 (2013): 415–423.

Chenoweth, Erica, and Kurt Schock. "Do Contemporaneous Armed Challenges Affect the Outcomes of Mass Nonviolent Campaigns?" *Mobilization: An International Quarterly* 20, no. 4 (2015): 427–451.

Chenoweth, Erica, and Christopher Shay. "Updating Nonviolent Campaigns: Introducing NAVCO 2.1." Paper presented at the *American Political Science Association Annual Conference, San Francisco, CA, August 31, 2017.*

Chenoweth, Erica, and Maria J. Stephan. *Why Civil Resistance Works: The Strategic Logic of Nonviolent Conflict.* New York, NY: Columbia University Press, 2011.

Chenoweth, Erica, and Maria J. Stephan. *The Role of External Support in Nonviolent Campaigns: Poisoned Chalice or Holy Grail?* Washington, DC: ICNC Press, 2021.

Clark, Howard. *Campaigning Power and Civil Courage: Bringing 'People Power' Back into Conflict Transformation.* London: Committee for Conflict Transformation Support, 2005**.**

Codur, Anne-Marie, and Mary Elizabeth King. "2015". "Women in Civil Resistance." In *Women, War and Violence: Typography, Resistance and Hope*, edited by Mariam M. Kurtz and Lester R. Kurtz, 401–446. Santa Barbara, CA: Praeger, 2015.

Collier, Paul, V. L. Elliott, Håvard Hegre, Anke Hoeffler, Marta Reynal-Querol, and Nicholas Sambanis. *Breaking the Conflict Trap: Civil War and Development Policy.* New York, NY: World Bank Publications and Oxford University Press, 2003.

Collier, Paul, Anke Hoeffler, and Måns Söderbom. "Post-Conflict Risks." *Journal of Peace Research* 45, no. 4 (2008): 461–478.

Coppedge, Michael, et al. "V-Dem Dataset v7." Varieties of Democracy (V-Dem) Project, 2017. **https://doi.org/10.23696/vdemcy17**.

Cunningham, Kathleen Gallagher. "Understanding Strategic Choice: The Determinants of Civil War and Nonviolent Campaign in Self-Determination Disputes." *Journal of Peace Research* 50 no. 3 (2013): 291–304.

Dahl, Marianne, Scott Gates, Kristian S. Gleditsch, and Belén González. "Accounting for Numbers: How Group Characteristics Shape the Choice of Violent and Non-Violent Tactics." Oslo, Norway: Peace Research Institute Oslo, 2018.

Dahl, Robert A. *Polyarchy: Participation and Opposition.* New Haven, CT: Yale University Press, 1971.

Davenport, Christian. *How Social Movements Die: Repression and Demobilization of the Republic of New Africa*. Cambridge: Cambridge University Press, 2014.

DeNardo, James. *Power in Numbers: The Political Strategy of Protest and Rebellion*. Princeton, NJ: Princeton University Press, 1985.

De Rouen, Jr., Karl, Jacob Bercovitch, and Paulina Pospieszna. Introducing the Civil Wars Mediation (CWM) Dataset." *Journal of Peace Research* 48, no. 5 (2011): 663–672.

Doyle, Michael W., and Nicholas Sambanis. *Making War and Building Peace: United Nations Peace Operations*. Princeton, NJ: Princeton University Press, 2006.

Dudouet, Véronique. *Peacemaking and Nonviolent Resistance. A Study of the Complementarity between Conflict Resolution Processes and Nonviolent Intervention, with Special Reference to the Case of Israel-Palestine*. PhD Dissertation. Bradford, England: University of Bradford, 2005.

Dudouet, Véronique. "Nonviolent Resistance in Power Asymmetries." In *Advancing Conflict Transformation: The Berghof Handbook II*, edited by Beatrix Austin, Martina Fischer and Hans J. Giessmann. Birmingham, England: Barbara Budrich Publishers, 2011.

Dudouet, Véronique. "Conflict Transformation through Nonviolent Resistance". In *Conflict Transformation: Essays on Methods of Nonviolence*, edited by Rhea DuMont, Tom H. Hastings, and Emiko Noma. Jefferson, NC: McFarland & Company Publishers, 2013.

Dudouet, Véronique. *Powering to Peace: Integrated Civil Resistance and Peacebuilding Strategies*. Washington, DC: ICNC Press, 2017. **https://www.nonviolent-conflict.org/powering-peace-integrated-civil-resistance-peacebuilding-strategies/**.

Dudouet, Véronique. "People Power and Peace Processes: Role and Impact of Nonviolent Collective Action by Grassroots social Movements on Civil War Resolution." Paper presented at *USIP workshop on Nonviolent Movements and Peace Processes, July 2019*.

Francis, Diana. *People, Peace and Power: Conflict Transformation in Action*. London, England: Pluto Press, 2002.

Francis, Diana. "Conflict Transformation: A Global Agenda." Report of the Committee for Conflict Transformation Support Number 41, December 2009. **https://rc-services-assets. s3.eu-west-1.amazonaws.com/s3fs-public/ Review41.pdf**.

Fortna, Virginia Page. *Does Peacekeeping Work?: Shaping Belligerents' Choices after Civil War*. Princeton, NJ: Princeton University Press, 2008.

Funari, Ellen, Huibert Oldenhuis, and Rachel Julian. "Securing Space for Local Peacebuilding: the Role of International and National Civilian Peacekeepers." *Peacebuilding* 3, no. 3 (2015): 297–313.

Galvanek, Janel B., and James Suah Shilue. *Working Tirelessly for Peace and Equality: Civil Resistance and Peacebuilding in Liberia*. Washington, DC: ICNC Press, 2021. **https:// www.nonviolent-conflict.org/resource/working-tirelessly-for-peace-and-equality-civil-resistance-and-peacebuilding-in-liberia-sr/**.

Gates, Scott, Håvard Mokleiv Nygård and Esther Trappeniers. "Conflict Recurrence." *Conflict Trends* 2. Oslo, Norway: PRIO, 2016. **https://www.prio.org/Publications/Publication/?x=9056**.

Goldstone, Jack A. *Revolution and Rebellion in the Early Modern World: Population Change and State Breakdown in England, France, Turkey, and China, 1600–1850*. Berkeley, CA: University of California Press, 1991.

George, Alexander L., and Andrew Bennett. *Case Studies and Theory Development in the Social Sciences.* Cambridge, MA: MIT Press, 2004.

Gleditsch, Kristian S., and Michael D. Ward. "Diffusion and the International Context of Democratization." *International Organization* 60, no. 4 (2006): 911–933.

Gleditsch, Nils Petter, Peter Wallensteen, Mikael Eriksson, Margareta Sollenberg, and Håvard Strand. "Armed Conflict 1946–2001: A New Dataset." *Journal of Peace Research* 39, no. 5 (2002): 615–637.

Guelke, Adrian. *Rethinking the Rise and Fall of Apartheid: South Africa and World Politics.* New York: Palgrave Macmillan, 2005.

Hallward, Maia, Juan Masullo, and Cécile Mouly. "Civil Resistance in Armed Conflict: Leveraging Nonviolent Action to Navigate War, Oppose Violence and Confront Oppression." *Journal of Peacebuilding & Development* 12, no. 3 (2017): 1–9.

Hancock, Landon, and Christopher Mitchell. *Zones of Peace.* Sterling, VA: Kumarian Press, 2007.

Hartzell, Caroline, and Matthew Hoddie. "Institutionalizing Peace: Power Sharing and Post-Civil War Conflict Management." *American Journal of Political Science* 47, no. 2 (2003): 318–332.

Hegre, Håvard, Tanja Ellingsen, Scott Gates, and Nils Petter Gleditsch. "Toward a Democratic Civil Peace? Democracy, Political Change, and Civil War, 1816–1992." *American Political Science Review* 95, no. 1 (2001): 33–48.

Hegre, Håvard, Lisa Hultman, and Håvard M. Nygård. "Evaluating the Conflict-Reducing Effect of UN Peacekeeping Operations." *Journal of Politics.* 81, no. 1 (2019): 215–232.

Hegre, Håvard, and Håvard M. Nygård. "Governance and Conflict Relapse." *Journal of Conflict Resolution* 59, no. 6 (2015): 984–1016.

Johnstad, Petter G. "Nonviolent Democratization: A Sensitivity Analysis of How Transition Mode and Violence Impact the Durability of Democracy." *Peace & Change* 35, no. 3 (2010): 464–482.

Julian, Rachel, and Christine Schweitzer. "The Origins and Development of Unarmed Civilian Peacekeeping." *Peace Review* 27, no. 1 (2015): 1–8.

Kaplan, Oliver. "Nudging Armed Groups: How Civilians Transmit Norms of Protection." *Stability: International Journal of Security and Development* 2, no. 3 (2013a): 62. **http://doi.org/10.5334/sta.cw**

Kaplan, Oliver. "Protecting Civilians in Civil War: The Institution of the ATCC in Colombia." *Journal of Peace Research* 50, no. 3 (2013b): 351–367.

Kaplin, Oliver. *Resisting War: How Communities Protect Themselves.* Cambridge, MA: Cambridge University Press, 2017.

Karatnycky, Adrian, and Peter Ackerman. "How Freedom Is Won: From Civic Resistance to Durable Democracy." *International Journal of Not-for-Profit Law* 7, no. 3 (2005).

Karis, Thomas. "Black Politics: The Road to Revolution." In *Apartheid in Crisis*, edited by Mark A. Uhlig. New York, NY: Vantage Books, 1986.

Keck, Margaret E., and Kathryn Sikkink. *Activists Beyond Borders.* Ithaca, NY: Cornell University Press, 1998.

Kirby Coel, and Christina Murray. "Elusive Autonomy in Sub-Saharan Africa." In *Asymmetric Autonomy and the Settlement of Ethnic Conflicts*, edited by Marc Weller and Katherine Nobbs. Philadelphia: University of Pennsylvania Press, 2010.

Koefoed, Minoo. "Constructive Resistance in Northern Kurdistan: Exploring the Peace, Development and Resistance Nexus." *Journal of Peacebuilding & Development* 12, no. 3 (2017): 39–53.

Kreutz, Joakim. "How and When Armed Conflicts End: Introducing the UCDP Conflict Termination Dataset." *Journal of Peace Research* 47, no. 2 (2010): 243–250.

Kriesberg, Louis. *Constructive Conflicts: From Escalation to Resolution*. Lanham, MD: Rowman & Littlefield, 2003.

Kriesberg, Louis, and Bruce W. Dayton. *Constructive Conflicts: From Escalation to Resolution*. 4th ed. Lanham, MD: Rowman & Littlefield, 2012.

Kurtz, Lester R. *The Anti-Apartheid Struggle in South Africa (1912–1992)*. Washington, DC: ICNC, 2009. **https://www.nonviolent-conflict. org/wp-content/uploads/2019/03/South-Africa-Anti-Apartheid-Summary.pdf**.

Lederach, John Paul. *Preparing For Peace: Conflict Transformation Across Cultures*. New York, NY: Syracuse University Press, 1995.

Lederach, John Paul. *Building Peace: Sustainable Reconciliation in Divided Societies*. Washington, DC: USIP, 1997.

Lehoucq, Fabrice. "Does Nonviolence Work?" *Comparative Politics* 48, no. 2 (2016): 269–87.

Leventoğlu, Bahar, and Nils W. Metternich. "Born Weak, Growing Strong: Anti‑Government Protests as a Signal of Rebel Strength in the Context of Civil Wars." *American Journal of Political Science* 62, no. 3 (2018): 581–596.

Levitsky, Steven, and Lucan A. Way. *Competitive Authoritarianism: Hybrid Regimes After the Cold War*. Cambridge, MA: Cambridge University Press, 2010.

Lieberman, Evan S. "Nested Analysis as a Mixed-Method Strategy for Comparative Research." *American Political Science Review* 99, no. 3 (2005): 435–452.

Lode, Kåre. "Mali's Peace Process: Context, Analysis and Evaluation." In *Owning the Process: Public Participation in Peacemaking (Conciliation Resources Accord Series),* edited by Catherine Barnes. London: Conciliation Resources, 2002. **https://www.c-r.org/accord/public-participation/malis-peace-process-context-analysis-and-evaluation**.

Lodge, Tom. "The Interplay of Non-violent and Violent Action in the Movement against Apartheid in South Africa, 1983–94." In *Civil Resistance and Power Politics,* edited by Adam Roberts and Timothy Garton Ash. Oxford, England: Oxford University Press, 2011.

Masullo, Juan. *The Power of Staying Put: Nonviolent Resistance Against Armed Groups in Colombia*. Washington, DC: ICNC Press, 2015. **https://www.nonviolent-conflict.org/wp-content/uploads/2016/01/The-Power-of-Staying-Put.pdf**.

McAllister, Pam. "You Can't Kill the Spirit: Women and Nonviolent Action." In *Nonviolent Social Movements: A Geographical Perspective*, edited by Stephen Zunes, Sarah Beth Asher, and Lester R. Kurtz. Oxford, England: Blackwell, 1999.

Mouly, Cécile, María Belén Garrido, and Annette Idler. "How Peace Takes Shape Locally: The Experience of Civil Resistance in Samaniego, Colombia." *Peace and Change* 41, no. 2 (2018): 129–166.

Mouly, Cécile, Annette Idler, and Belén Garrido. "Zones of Peace in Colombia's Borderlands." *International Journal of Peace Studies* 20, no. 1 (2015): 51–63.

Nepstad, Sharon. *Nonviolent Revolutions: Civil Resistance in the Late 20th Century*. Oxford, England: Oxford University Press, 2011.

New Humanitarian. "A Timeline of Northern Conflict." 2012. **http://www.thenewhumanitarian.org/report/95252/mali-timeline-northern-conflict**.

Nilsson, Desirée. "Anchoring the Peace: Civil Society Actors in Peace Accords and Durable Peace." *International Interactions* 38, no. 2 (2012): 243–266.

O'Donnell, Guillermo, and Philippe C. Schmitter. *Transitions from Authoritarian Rule, vol. 4: Tentative Conclusions about Uncertain Democracies.* Baltimore, MD: Johns Hopkins University Press, 1986.

Olzak, Susan, and Emily Ryo. "Organizational Diversity, Vitality and Outcomes in the Civil Rights Movement." *Social Forces* 85, no. 4 (2007): 1561–1591.

Passanante, Aly, and Max Rennebohm. "Malians Defeat Dictator, Gain Free Election (March Revolution), 1991." *Global Nonviolent Action Database.* 2011. **https://nvdatabase.swarthmore.edu/content/malians-defeat-dictator-gain-free-election-march-revolution-1991**.

Paxton, Pamela, Melanie M. Hughes, and Jennifer L. Green. "The International Women's Movement and Women's Political Representation, 1893–2003." *American Sociological Review* 71 (2006): 898–920.

Pearlman, Wendy. *Violence, Nonviolence, and the Palestinian National Movement.* Cambridge, England: Cambridge University Press, 2011.

Perkoski, Evan, and Erica Chenoweth. *Nonviolent Resistance and Prevention of Mass Killings During Popular Uprisings.* Washington, DC: ICNC Press, 2018. **https://www.nonviolent-conflict.org/nonviolent-resistance-and-prevention-of-mass-killings/**.

Pettersson, Thérése, and Peter Wallensteen. "Armed Conflicts, 1946–2014." *Journal of Peace Research* 52, no. 4 (2015): 536–550.

Pinckney, Jonathan. *Making or Breaking Nonviolent Discipline in Civil Resistance Movements.* Washington, DC: ICNC Press, 2016. **https://www.nonviolent-conflict.org/making-or-breaking-nonviolent-discipline-in-civil-resistance-movements/**.

Pinckney, Jonathan. *When Civil Resistance Succeeds: Building Democracy After Popular Nonviolent Uprising.* Washington, DC: ICNC Press, 2018. **https://www.nonviolent-conflict.org/wp-content/uploads/2018/10/When-Civil-Resistance-Succeeds-Pinckney-monograph.pdf**.

Pinckney, Jonathan. *How to Win Well: Civil Resistance Breakthroughs and the Path to Democracy.* Washington, DC: ICNC Press, 2021. **https://www.nonviolent-conflict.org/wp-content/uploads/2021/04/Pinckney_SR_How_To_Win_Well.pdf**

Pinckney, Jonathan, Charles R. Butcher, and Jessica M. Braithwaite. (2019). "Durability not Diversity: Uncovering the Organizational Roots of Democratization." Working Paper.

Popovic, Srdja, and Matthew Miller. *Blueprint for Revolution: How to Use Rice Pudding, Lego Men, and Other Nonviolent Techniques to Galvanize Communities, Overthrow Dictators, or Simply Change the World.* New York: Spiegel and Grau, 2015.

Przeworski, Adam. *Democracy and the Market: Political and Economic Reforms in Eastern Europe and Latin America.* Cambridge, England: Cambridge University Press, 1991.

Quinn, J. Michael, T. David Mason, and Mehmet Gurses. "Sustaining the Peace: Determinants of Civil War Recurrence." *International Interactions* 33, no. 2 (2007): 167–193.

Price, Robert M. *The Apartheid State in Crisis: Political Transformations in South Africa, 1975–1990.* Oxford, England: Oxford University Press, 1991.

Principe, Marie A. *Women in Nonviolent Movements.* USIP Special Report, No. 399. Washington, DC: USIP, 2017. **https://www.usip.org/sites/default/files/SR399-Women-in-Nonviolent-Movements.pdf**.

Randle, Michael. *Civil Resistance.* London, England: Fontana Press, 1994.

Ritter, Daniel P. *The Iron Cage of Liberalism: International Politics and Unarmed Revolutions in the Middle East and North Africa.* New York, NY: Oxford University Press, 2014.

Robson, David. "The '3.5% Rule': How a Small Minority Can Change the World." *BBC News.* 13 May 2019. **http://www.bbc.com/future/story/20190513-it-only-takes-35-of-people-to-change-the-world**.

Saraceno, Francesco. "Reflections on Azawad Crisis and Malian Democracy: The Statehood, its Deficiencies and Inclusion Failure." *Journal of Asian and African Studies* 50, no. 3 (2015): 343–358.

Schirch, Lisa. *Little Book of Strategic Peacebuilding: A Vision and Framework for Peace with Justice.* New York, NY: Good Books, 2005.

Schock, Kurt. *Unarmed Insurrections: People Power Movements in Nondemocracies.* Minneapolis, MN: University of Minnesota Press, 2005.

Seekings, Jeremy. *The UDF: A History of the United Democratic Front in South Africa, 1983–1991.* Athens, OH: Ohio University Press, 2000.

Sharp, Gene. *The Politics of Nonviolent Action.* Boston, MA: Porter Sargent Publishers, 1973.

Smith, Zeric Kay. "Francophone Africa in Flux: Mali's Decade of Democracy." *Journal of Democracy,* 12, no. 3 (2001): 73–79.

Smuts, Dene, and Shauna Westcott. *The Purple Shall Govern: A South African A to Z of Nonviolent Action.* Oxford, England: Oxford University Press, 1999.

Stigant, Susan, and Elizabeth Murray. *National Dialogues: A Tool for Conflict Transformation?* USIP Peace Brief 194. Washington, DC: USIP, 2015. **https://www.usip.org/publications/2015/10/national-dialogues-tool-conflict-transformation**.

Subedi, D. B., and Prakash Bhattarai. "The April Uprising: How a Nonviolent Struggle Explains the Transformation of Armed Conflict in Nepal." *Journal of Peacebuilding & Development* 12, no. 3 (2017): 85–97.

Swilling, Mark. "The United Democratic Front and Township Revolt." In *Popular Struggles in South Africa,* edited by William Cobbett and Robin Cohen. Trenton, NJ: Africa World Press, 1988.

Teorell, Jan. *Determinants of Democratization: Explaining Regime Change in the World, 1972–2006.* Cambridge, England: Cambridge University Press, 2010.

Thompson, Leonard. *A History of South Africa (3rd Edition).* London, England: Yale University Press, 2001.

Turrittin, J. "Mali: People Topple Traoré." *Review of African Political Economy* 52 (1991): 97–103.

Ulfelder, Jay. "Contentious Collective Action and the Breakdown of Authoritarian Regimes." *International Political Science Review* 26, no. 3 (2005): 311–334.

Ulfelder, Jay. *Dilemmas of Democratic Consolidations: A Game-Theory Approach.* Boulder, CO: First Forum, 2010.

Ulfelder, Jay. "Democracy/Autocracy Data Set (DAD) Handbook." Harvard Dataverse, V1. 2012. **http://hdl.handle.net/1902.1/18836**.

United Nations. *National Covenant of Republic of Mali's Nord Pact*. Signed April 11, 1992. **https://peacemaker.un.org/mali-pacte-reconciliation-national92**.

Uppsala Conflict Data Program. *UCDP Conflict Encyclopedia*. 2019. **www.ucdp.uu.se**.

Vanhanen, Tatu. *The Process of Democratization: A Comparative Study of 147 States, 1980–88*. New York, NY: Crane Russak, 1990.

Vengroff, Richard. "Governance and the Transition to Democracy: Political Parties and the Party System in Mali." *Journal of Modern African Studies* 31, no. 4 (1993): 541–562.

Vengroff, Richard, and Moctar Kone. "Mali: Democracy and Political Change." *Democracy and Political Change in Sub-Saharan Africa*, edited by John A. Wiseman. London, England: Taylor and Francis, 1995.

Vüllers, Johannes, and Roman Krtsch. "Raise Your Voices! Civilian Protest in Civil Wars." *Political Geography* 80 (2020): 1–12.

Walter, Barbara F. *Committing to Peace: The Successful Settlement of Civil Wars*. Princeton, NJ: Princeton University Press, 2002.

Walter, Barbara F. "Does Conflict Beget Conflict? Explaining Recurring Civil War." *Journal of Peace Research* 41, no. 3 (2004): 371–388.

Wanis-St. John, Anthony, and Noah Rosen. *Negotiating Civil Resistance*. USIP Special Report. Washington, DC: USIP, 2017. **https://www.usip.org/publications/2017/07/negotiating-civil-resistance**.

Ward, Michael D., Brian D. Greenhill, and Kristin M. Bakke. "The Perils of Policy by P-Value: Predicting Civil Conflicts." *Journal of Peace Research* 47, no. 4 (2010): 363–375.

White, Peter B., Dragana Vidovic, Belén González, Kristian S. Gleditsch and David E. Cunningham. "Nonviolence as a Weapon of the Resourceful: From Claims to Tactics in Mobilization." *Mobilization: An International Quarterly* 20, no. 4 (2015): 471–491.

Wing, Susanna D. "Mali: Politics of Crisis." *African Affairs* 112, no. 448 (2013): 476–485.

World Bank. *World Development Indicators*. 2016. **http://data.worldbank.org/data-catalog/world-development-indicators**.

Zunes, Stephen. "The Role of Non-Violent Action in the Downfall of Apartheid." *Journal of Modern African Studies* 37, no. 1 (1999): 137–169.

Zunes, Stephen. "Mali's Struggle: Not Simply of Their Own Making" *Open Democracy*. 11 May 2012. **https://www.opendemocracy.net/en/malis-struggle-not-simply-of-their-own-making-0/**.

Zunes, Stephen. *Sudan's 2019 Revolution: The Power of Civil Resistance*. Washington, DC: ICNC Press, 2021. **https://www.nonviolent-conflict.org/resource/sudans-2019-revolution-the-power-of-civil-resistance/**.

Zunes, Stephen, and Katherine Nesbitt. "Mali's March Revolution (1991)." Washington, DC: ICNC, 2009. **https://www.nonviolent-conflict.org/malis-march-revolution-1991/**.

Appendix I: Methodological Approach

This methodological appendix describes in much greater detail the research methods that underpinned the quantitative findings and how these methods work, as well as the data that was used to account for potentially favorable conditions for nonviolent resistance and alternative explanations in each of the statistical models (i.e., the control variables). The following sections in the appendix provide a more detailed report of the quantitative findings and include all the variables used in each regression model. This appendix specifically aims at a scholarly audience but may be of interest to a general reader that is curious about the methods undertaken in this monograph.

Statistical Approach and How It Works

Because each dependent variable is binary, the primary statistical method used is logistic regression models. Regression models report a coefficient and a p-value. The coefficient tells us about the direction and nature of the relationship between the independent variables (predictors) and dependent variable (outcome). All propositions in this study are testing against the null hypothesis (the notion that our proposed relationships could have only occurred by chance). The p-value can be interpreted as the predicted likelihood that a relationship did not occur by chance. The minimum threshold used in political science is a p-value of 0.05, which implies that we can be 95 percent certain that the observed relationship is statistically significant and has not simply occurred by chance.[37]

This study also uses Cox proportional hazards models. These models differ in that they look at the duration, or "survival," of a particular outcome until a new outcome emerges. For instance, in the case of civil war, such models assess the survival of civil war and the time until the civil war is terminated by a negotiated agreement. Similarly, in the post-conflict phase, this model calculates the survival of peace until a point in time in which conflict reoccurs.

In-Sample and Out-of-Sample Prediction and How It Works

While logistic regression allows us to explore the relationship between independent variables and dependent variables, the extent of the relationship is difficult to interpret directly. In logistic models, a higher coefficient does not necessarily indicate a stronger effect relative

---

37   Standard errors, which measure the statistical accuracy of the model, are clustered by conflict episodes to account for the fact that conflict episodes are different from one another.

to other variables. In order to understand the substantive marginal effects, it is necessary to run in-sample predictive simulations, comparing the predictive probability of the outcome for cases where nonviolent campaigns are present with cases where they are not.

Out-of-sample prediction serves as a harder test for the predictive power of a model and can better assess whether key variables increase or reduce predictive power (Ward Greenhill, and Bakke 2010). This involves using in-sample predictions from seen data (i.e., training data) to explain outcomes in data that has not been seen (i.e., test data). K-fold cross-validation is used in this study using four k-folds—learning from three random segments of the data to predict a final fourth test segment of the data.[38] The output reports the size of area under the curve (AUC), which ranges from 1.0 (perfectly predictive) and 0.5 (non-predictive). Higher rates have lower false positive and higher true positive outcomes.

Control Variables

Statistical analyses allow to account for alternative explanations by including control variables in the models. For the statistical analysis of civil war episodes (Stage 1), a number of controls that impact and may explore the termination of civil war and viability of nonviolent campaigns are included in the analysis. This includes GDP per capita (logged) and national population (logged).[39] Problems of coordinating activists are reduced in industrialized and urbanized states (Goldstone 1991), and larger countries are more prone to nonviolent and violent dissent. Regime type is also controlled for using V-Dem's Country Polyarchy Score with a scale from 0 (least democratic) to 1 (most democratic) based on five dimensions: freedom of expression, freedom of association, free elections, fairness of those elections, and proportion of the population that can vote (Coppedge et al. 2017).[40] Autocracies are more likely to repress all forms of dissent which can impact nonviolent mobilization and exacerbate armed conflict.

Next, a number of variables relating to the nature of the civil war are included: conflict intensity (number of UCDP battlefield deaths (logged)), the type of conflict (territorial or government-based), and the number of civil war years can impact the likelihood of peace. Finally, a dummy variable is included for third-party mediation attempts (DeRouen, Bercovitch, and Pospieszna 2011) and the presence of UN peacekeeping missions (more robust Chapter 7 missions with enforcement mandates) as external interventions (Hegre, Hultman, and Nygard

---

38   Ten folds in k cross-validation is the norm in the machine learning literature and with large datasets. However, the sample sizes in this study are relatively much smaller.

39   Regression models assume a linear relationship between independent variables and the outcome. Logging a variable helps to account for non-linear relationships. Data is taken from the World Bank (2016).

40   For more information, see the Varieties of Democracy codebook at **https://www.v-dem.net/en/data/dataversion-7/**.

2019) may explain why peace has occurred and may provide more favorable conditions for nonviolent resistance.

For the analysis of conflict recurrence, a number of controls are introduced to account for key alternative explanations of conflict recurrence, including prominent factors of poor economic development and poverty measured by GDP per capita (logged) (Quinn, Mason, and Gurses 2007; Collier, Hoeffler, and Sōderbom 2008), and weak institutions and levels of democracy as measured by V-Dem's Polyarchy Score (Walter 2004). To account for third-party interventions, controls are included for agreements that are brought about by mediation and for the presence of a peacekeeping mission, which significantly reduces the likelihood a conflict will reoccur (Fortna 2008). Also included is the intensity of the previous conflict (meaning the number of battle deaths) and the number of previous conflict years to account for a possible war weariness effect which reduces the likelihood civil war will reoccur (Walter 2004; Quinn et al. 2007). The time since last conflict is also included, as war begets war and most countries are most prone to conflict recurrence close to the previous civil war, with the average being seven years (Gates, Nygard, and Trappeniers 2016). To account for military involvement and influence in politics, which is associated with poor governance leading to civil war recurrence (Hegre and Nygard 2015), a control is included for a history of military rule. Finally, whether the past war was fought over the government or territory is also included, as territorial conflicts are harder to resolve.

For the analysis of post-conflict democratization, the nature of the previous civil war (i.e., intensity, type of conflict, and number of conflict years) and instances of third-party interventions in the previous conflict are included (i.e., third-party mediated talks). Third-party intervention such as mediation may increase the likelihood of democracy (i.e., mediated peace agreements often establish democratic principles as part of power sharing agreements, while peacekeepers may support democratic institutions and elections). Other prominent explanations for whether democratization is likely to occur include modernization theory whereby modernization creates greater demands for democratization (Teorell 2010), a history of military rule (Levitsky and Way 2010), and the diffusion of democracy (Gleditsch and Ward 2006). Controls for these explanations are added: whether military rule was evidenced in the previous armed conflict, GDP per capita, the percentage of the population that is urbanized, and the percentage of democracies within the region of a given country.

Appendix II: Detailed Statistical Results

This section provides the full results behind the predictions and data that are explored in Chapter 5 and in-sample and out-of-sample k-fold cross-validations that add further evidence for the propositions or hypotheses explored in this monograph.

This section follows the sequence of Chapter 5 in the main monograph: first, wartime nonviolent campaigns and negotiated civil war settlements outcomes (Stage 1); second, the impact these campaigns have on conflict recurrence and post-conflict democracy (Stage 2); and finally, the exploration of what attributes of nonviolent campaigns may explain the findings in both stages. Overall, in-sample and out-of-sample predictive analyses add further and consistent evidence to the findings found throughout the monograph.

Detailed Results of Stage 1: Nonviolent Campaigns and Civil War Agreements

In all analyses, if the coefficient (represented by the dot) is right of the red line, this represents a positive relationship with the outcome, while left of the line indicates a negative coefficient. The horizontal lines that reach out from the coefficient dots are the confidence intervals. If these confidence intervals overlap with the red line, then the result is not statistically significant, or in other words, less than 95 percent confidence that the result did not occur simply by chance. All variables related to nonviolent campaigns and third-party interventions in the civil war are lagged by one year to ensure casual ordering.[41]

---

41   This takes the values from the previous year, for instance, to ensure nonviolent campaigns were active prior to the signing of an agreement.

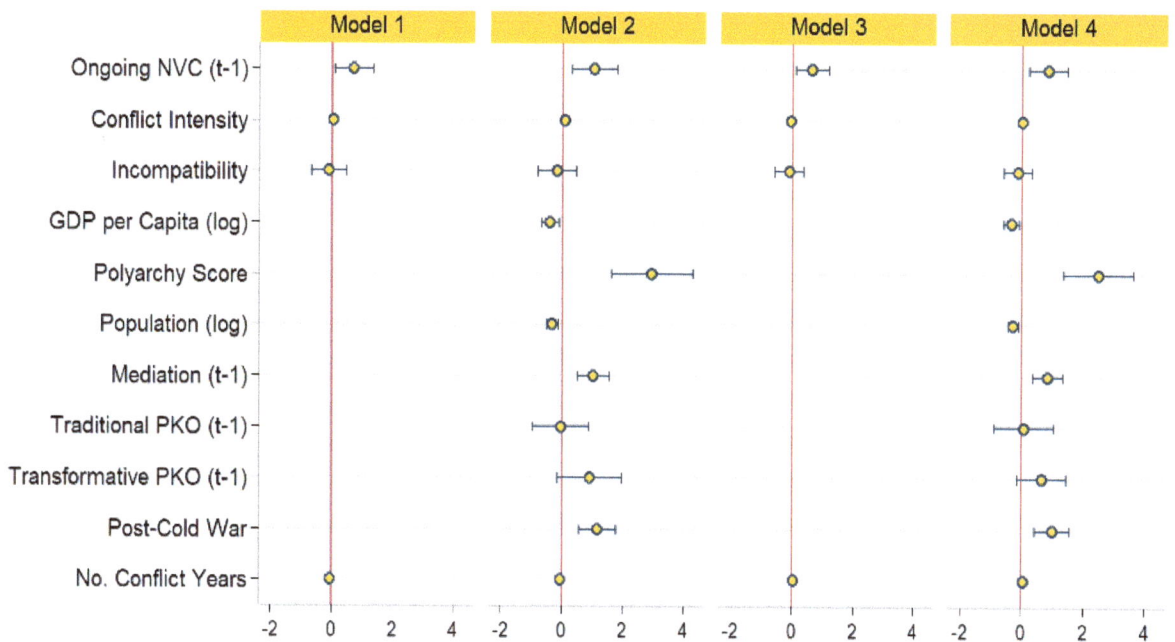

FIGURE 15. Logistic Regression and Cox Proportional Hazard Models:
Nonviolent Resistance and Negotiated Agreements (1955–2013)

Starting with the influence of nonviolent resistance during ongoing civil war, Figure 15 explores the likelihood of negotiated settlements given the presence of nonviolent campaigns. As Models 1–4 show, the coefficient is right of the red line, suggesting that the presence of largescale nonviolent resistance has a consistently positive impact on the negotiated resolution of civil war. When including control variables, the presence of wartime nonviolent campaigns still reports an independent effect on negotiated agreements. The confidence intervals (horizontal lines) do not overlap with the red line, which means these results are also statistically significant. As one would expect, more democratic regimes and civil wars that are mediated by third parties are also associated with greater chances for negotiated agreements, while more intense periods of civil war reduce the likelihood of an agreement.

Models 3 and 4 use alternative Cox proportional hazards models which instead assess the time it takes civil war to "fail" and to be terminated by a negotiated agreement. The positive coefficients in Models 3 and 4 can be interpreted as nonviolent campaigns increasing the likelihood civil war "failing" and being terminated by a negotiated agreement.[42] This

---

42   In these models, time-varying covariates are lagged by one year (t-1) and are appropriate for these models. Moreover, for ease of interpretation, the coefficient estimates are reported rather than the hazard ratios.

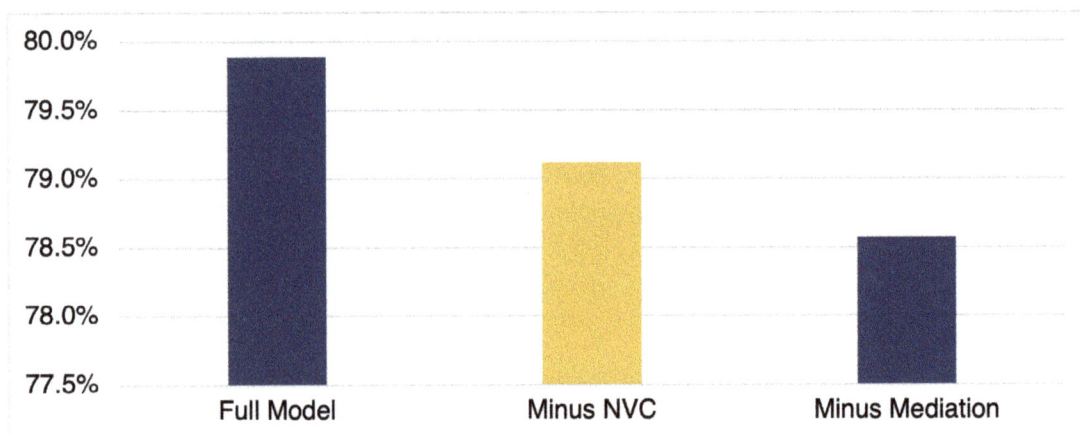

FIGURE 16. In-Sample Predictive Power: Nonviolent Campaigns (NVC) and Negotiated Settlements, based on data from 1955 to 2013

suggests nonviolent campaigns also reduce the duration of civil wars that end in a negotiated agreement.

Figure 16 explores the in-sample predictive power of the model, comparing the predictive power of the full logit regression model (recall Model 2 in Figure 1) with models that remove nonviolent campaigns and third-party mediation—one of the most common ways through which negotiated agreements are reached. Removing nonviolent campaigns from the full model reduces the predictive power of the model. This predictive power is further reduced when third-party mediation is removed from the full model. This suggests that third-party mediation is the factor most likely to bring about a peace agreement, which would be expected since mediation is the predominant way through which civil wars are resolved. Nevertheless, nonviolent campaigns are clearly also predictive of the outcome (negotiated settlements). As the statistical analysis shows, the effect of nonviolent campaigns is independent to the effect of mediation.

As a more stringent test, the predictive power is then explored out-of-sample, using k(4)-fold cross-validations (where three segments of the data are used to predict a final unseen segment of the data). Again, removing nonviolent campaigns and then mediation reduces the predictive power of the full model, with mediation being more predictive than nonviolent campaigns (see Figure 17). The predictive power of these models is a little lower in the out-of-sample than in the in-sample, which is encouraging given the fact that out-of-sample predictions constitute a much tougher test. The predictive analyses provide further evidence that nonviolent campaigns positively influence the peaceful settlement of civil wars.

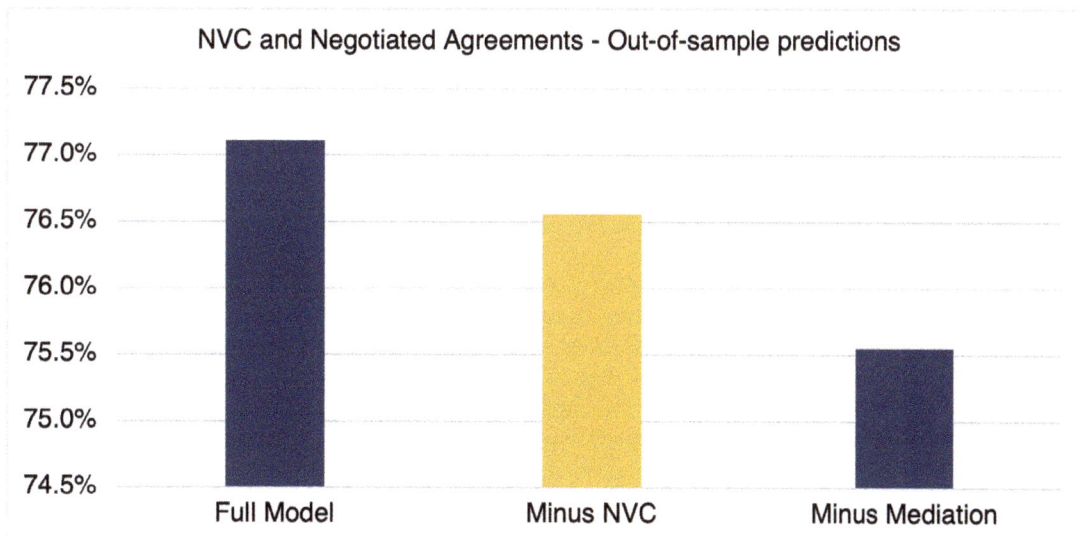

FIGURE 17. K-Fold Cross-Validation: Nonviolent Campaigns (NVC) and Negotiated Agreements, based on data from 1955 to 2013

Figures 13–16 provide strong statistical evidence for Proposition 1a, which argues that nonviolent campaigns have a positive impact on negotiated civil war agreements. The next section moves on to explore the post-conflict phase, conflict recurrence, and post-conflict democratization. It explores how likely it is for civil war to reoccur and for democratization to emerge after a civil war has come to an end, comparing whether a nonviolent movement was present in the previous civil war with cases where they were not.

Detailed Results of Stage 2a: Nonviolent Campaigns and Post-Conflict Conflict Recurrence

In Chapter 5, the results showed no relationship between nonviolent campaigns present in the previous civil war and the subsequent recurrence of armed conflict. Figure 18 reports the full findings: wartime nonviolent campaigns have no impact on the number of post-conflict peace years (i.e., durable peace—see Cox models) or the subsequent recurrence of civil war (see logit models). This provides little evidence for Proposition 1b. This also differs from previous findings that nonviolent campaigns reduce the likelihood of future civil war (Chenoweth and Stephan 2011; Johnstad 2010), although such studies did not specifically explore post-conflict years or countries with a recent history of civil war. Likewise, no statistically significant evidence is found that associates specific campaign attributes with a reduced likelihood of conflict recurrence.

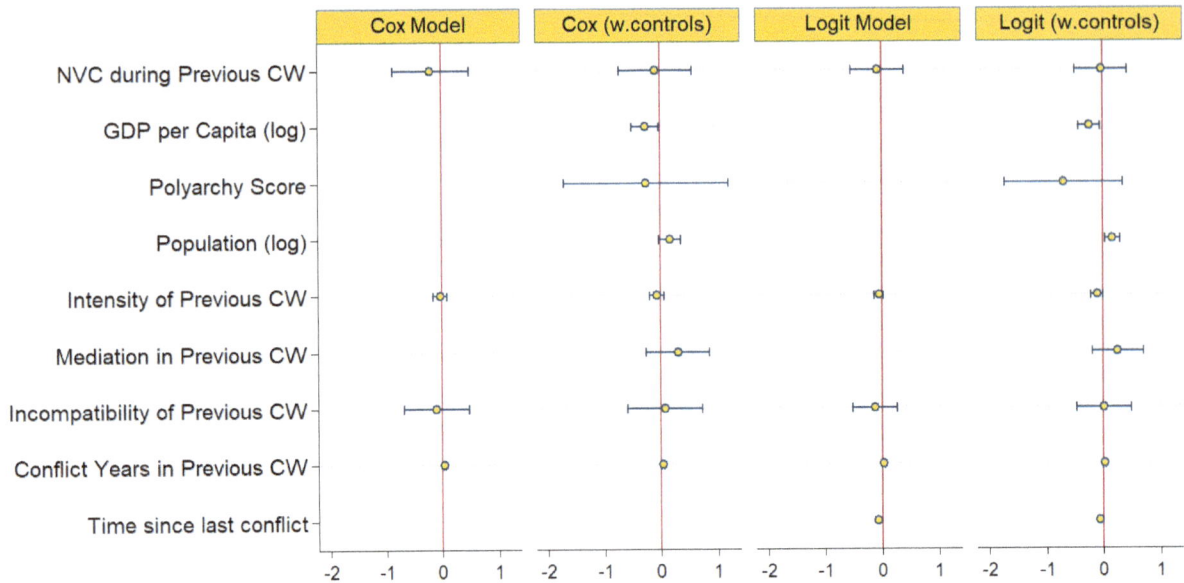

FIGURE 18. Cox Proportional Hazard and Logistic Regression Models: Nonviolent Campaigns (NVC) and the Recurrence of Civil War (1955–2013)

The most important determinant in Figure 18 is a previous history of civil war: countries with a history of war are much more prone to subsequent conflict than countries without a recent civil war. The presence of nonviolent campaigns does not appear to break this cycle of violence.

Detailed Results of Stage 2b:
Nonviolent Campaigns and Post-Conflict Democratization

The analysis moves on to explore post-conflict democratization and whether this is more likely when nonviolent campaigns were present in the previous civil war. Figure 19 reports the full logistic regression models and the various aspects of post-conflict democratic transitions. Across all models, the results consistently provide strong support to Proposition 1c, which argues that wartime nonviolent campaigns have a positive and statistically significant effect on the likelihood of post-conflict democratization. This effect increases in post-conflict years that are within five years of the last civil war (Democratization <5yrs). Finally, the effect is even stronger in post-conflict periods that proceed a negotiated settlement, which suggests in many cases that wartime nonviolent campaigns can both aid negotiated settlements and post-conflict democratization.

88

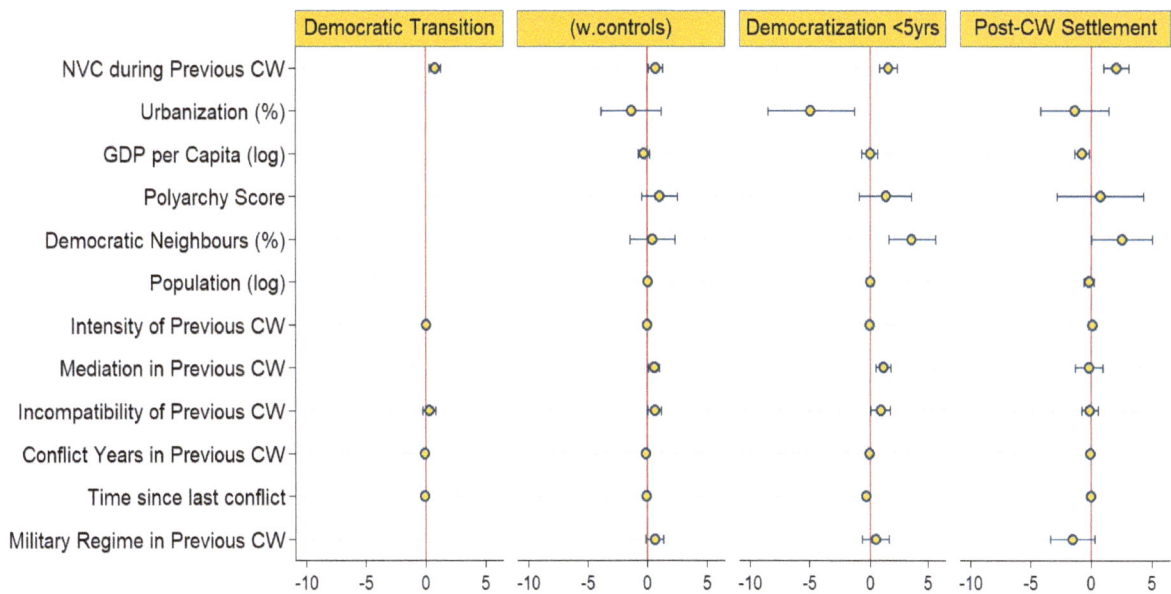

FIGURE 19. Logistic Regression Models: Nonviolent Campaigns (NVC) and Post-Conflict Democratic Transitions (1955–2010)

Following the approach taken in Stage 1 of the above analysis, the statistical results here are also supplemented with in- and out-of-sample predictive analyses, which test the predictive power of the model and key variables.

Figure 20 explores the in-sample predictive power of the logistic regression model (recall the first model in Figure 19) and compares the power of the full model with subsequent models that remove nonviolent campaigns (in the previous civil war), third party mediation (in the previous civil war), and democratic neighbors from the model. Removing any of these explanatory variables reduces the predictive power of the full model. The presence of nonviolent campaigns in the previous conflict is predictive, but as would be expected, is less predictive than wartime mediation and a higher number of democratic neighbors.

Figure 21 moves to the out-of-sample predictive analysis using k(4)-fold cross-validation (this methodology is explained in greater detail in Appendix I). Wartime nonviolent campaigns are predictive, as removing this variable reduces the predictive power of the model. Once again, previous mediation and more democratic neighbors are greater predictors of post-conflict democratization. And, again, the predictive power of this model is lower in the out-of-sample analysis than in the in-sample analysis, owing to the former being a tougher test.

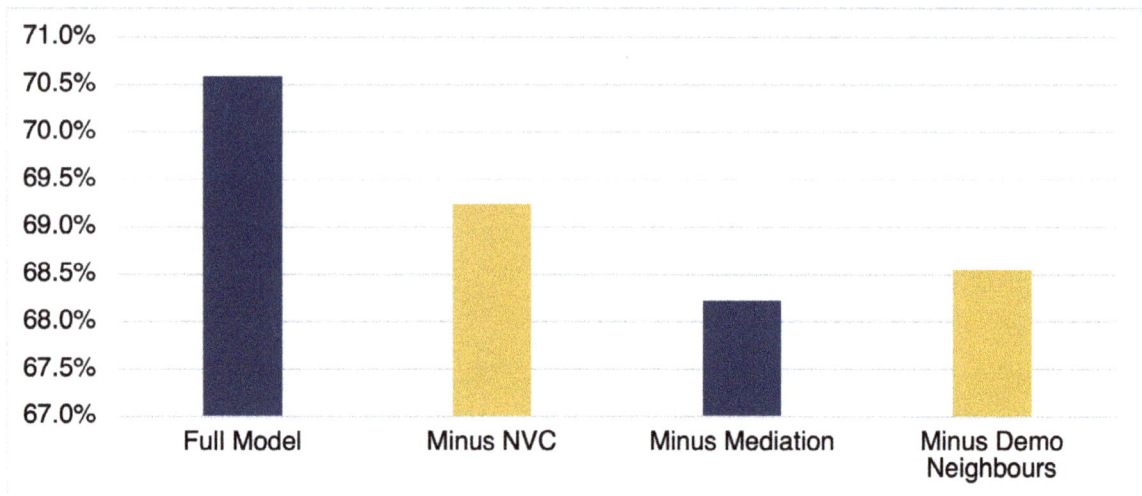

FIGURE 20. In-Sample Predictive Power: Nonviolent Campaigns (NVC) and Post-Conflict Democratization, based on data from 1955 to 2010

The next and final sections of this appendix explore the impact of campaign attributes on the outcomes presented above.

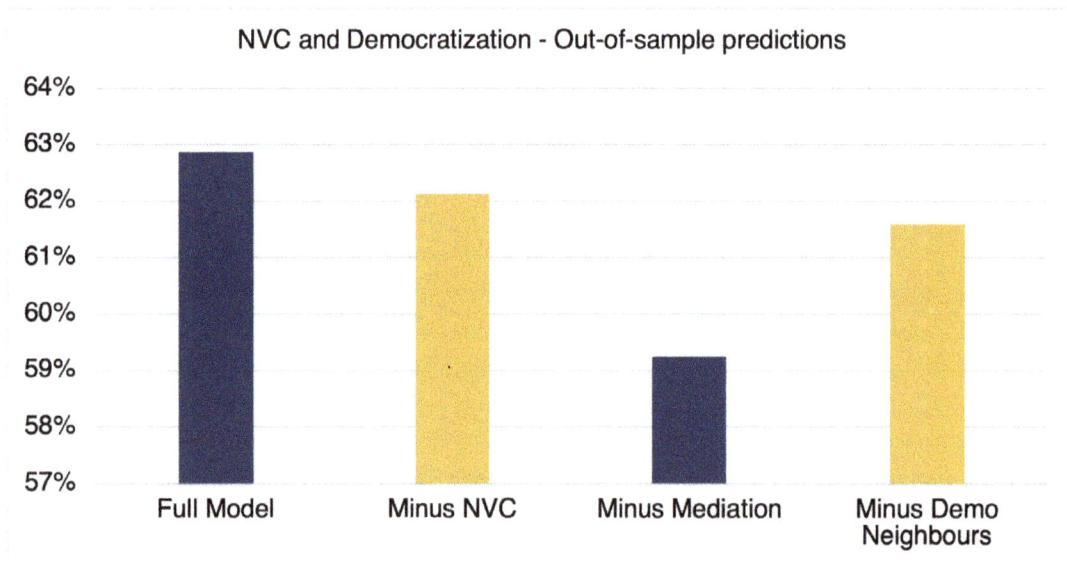

FIGURE 21. K-Fold Cross-Validation: Nonviolent Campaigns (NVC) and Democratic Transitions, based on data from 1955 to 2010

Detailed Results: Attributes of Nonviolent Campaigns and Negotiated Civil War Settlements

This final section of this appendix reports the impact of specific attributes of wartime nonviolent movements and whether this can help explain the greater likelihood of civil war agreements and post-conflict peace, starting with the comparison of nonviolent campaigns that are success with those that are not successful (see Figure 22). It is clear that successful campaigns are positively associated with negotiated agreements and that the effect is statistically significant—unlike that of failed campaigns, which have no effect.

According to the civil resistance literature, a key determinant of campaign success is the size of the campaign (number of participants). As Figure 22 shows, larger wartime nonviolent campaigns with greater participation have a positive and significant effect on negotiated agreements.

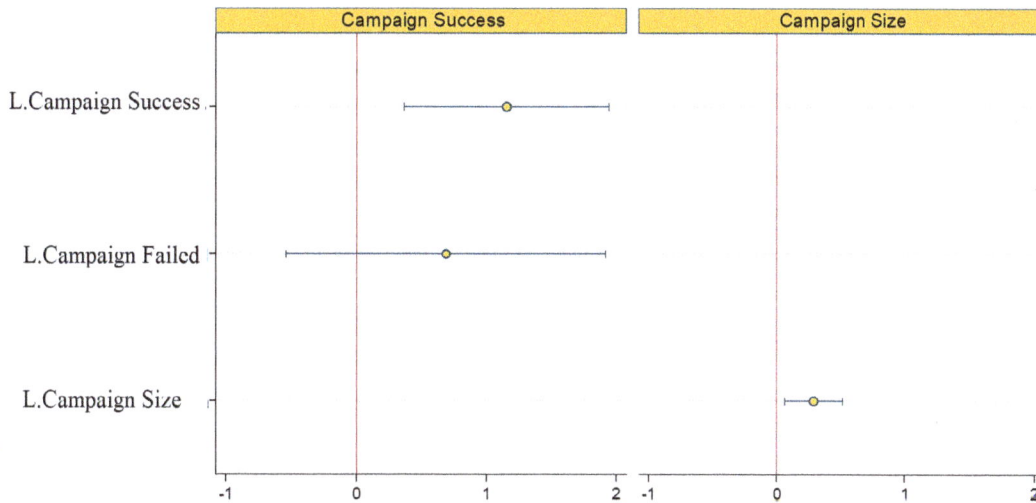

FIGURE 22. Logistic Regression Models: Campaign Success, Size, and Negotiated Agreements (1955–2013)

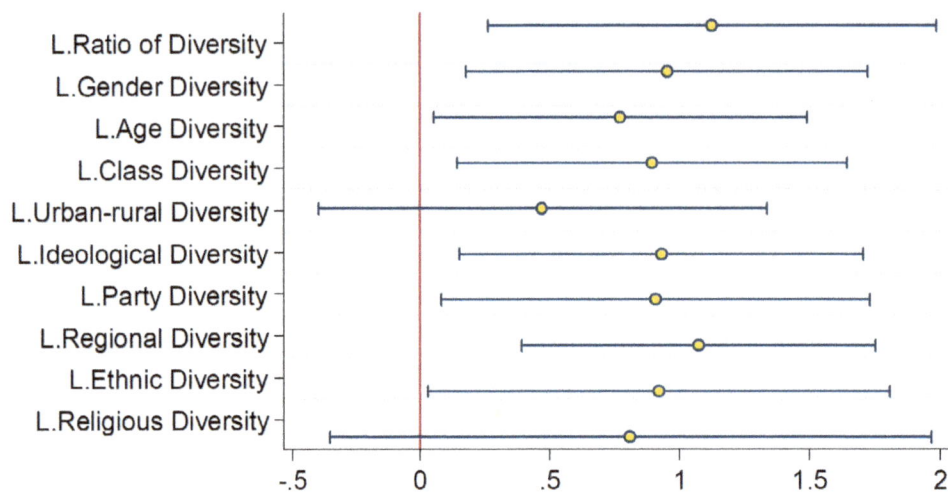

FIGURE 23. Logistic Regression Models: Campaign Diversity and Negotiated Agreements (1955–2013)

Turning to social diversity, Figure 23 presents the full results of a logistic regression model that explores the relationship between social diversity and negotiated settlements to civil wars.

A greater degree of social diversity within a wartime nonviolent movement (i.e., the ratio or score of diversity) reports the strongest coefficient and is therefore most associated with the likelihood of negotiated agreements. Overall, most forms of social diversity within a nonviolent campaign are positively associated with negotiated agreements, including ethnicity and ideology, which often form the basis of division within most civil wars. Interestingly, religious diversity has no significant effect. As was inferred in Proposition 5a, women's participation in the nonviolent movement is particularly important. Figure 9a (see page 43) shows that a negotiated agreement is twice as likely when movements are gender diverse, compared to campaigns that are not.

Figure 24 then reports the coefficients of other campaign features and the full models. Campaigns with a greater number of organizations and that development alternative institutions are associated with the greater likelihood of a negotiated agreement. While hierarchical leadership campaigns have no statistically significant effect, decentralized campaign structures do indeed appear to be more adaptable to civil war environments and positively impact negotiated settlements.

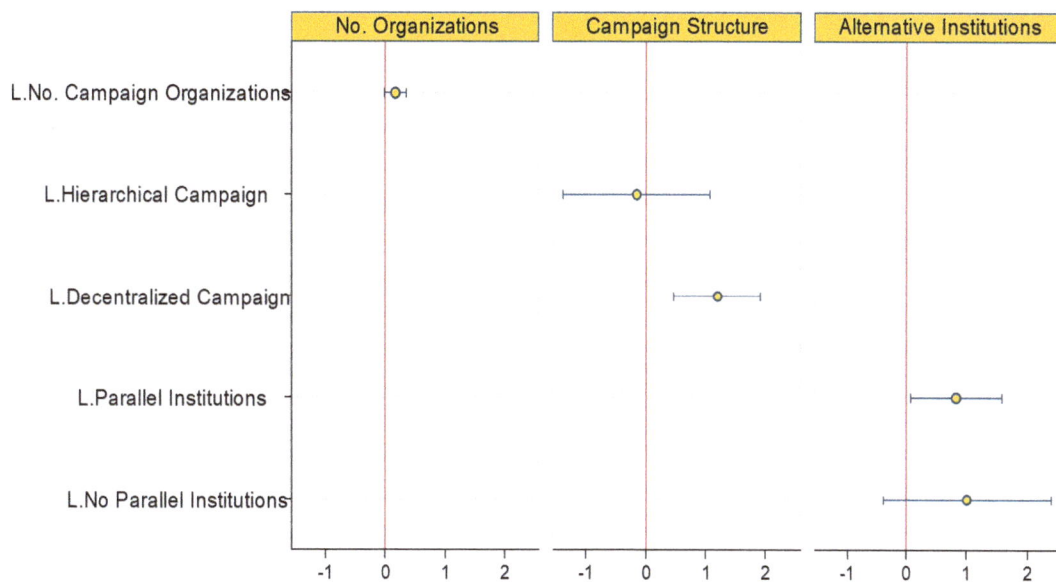

FIGURE 24. Logistic Regression Models: Other Attributes
and Negotiated Agreements (1955–2013)

As stated in the main text, these results provide clear evidence for **Propositions 2a–5a** and **7a–8a**. Campaign success, greater participation, movement diversity, alternative institutions and decentralized structure of a nonviolent campaign all increase the likelihood of a civil war ending in a negotiated settlement. However, Figure 24 shows that greater organizational diversity within campaigns has no statistically significant impact on settlements, meaning there is little support for **Proposition 6a**.

The cases of Mali and South Africa (explored in Chapter 6) show that a greater number of civil society organizations aided the resolution of civil war and led to fully comprehensive peace agreements. In these specific cases a diverse organizational membership provided the nonviolent movements with an organized and dispersed leadership that was adaptable to state repression. Yet this advantage is not reflected in other cases, as shown by the statistical analysis. It is likely that in other cases organizational diversity may create disunity, and such divisions may subsequently undermine the nonviolent campaign.

Detailed Results: Attributes of Nonviolent Campaigns and Post-Conflict Democratization

As discussed in the main analysis, the results from Figures 25 and 26 are almost identical to Figures 21–23: the specific features of nonviolent campaigns that aid the resolution of civil war are also strongly associated with post-conflict democratization.

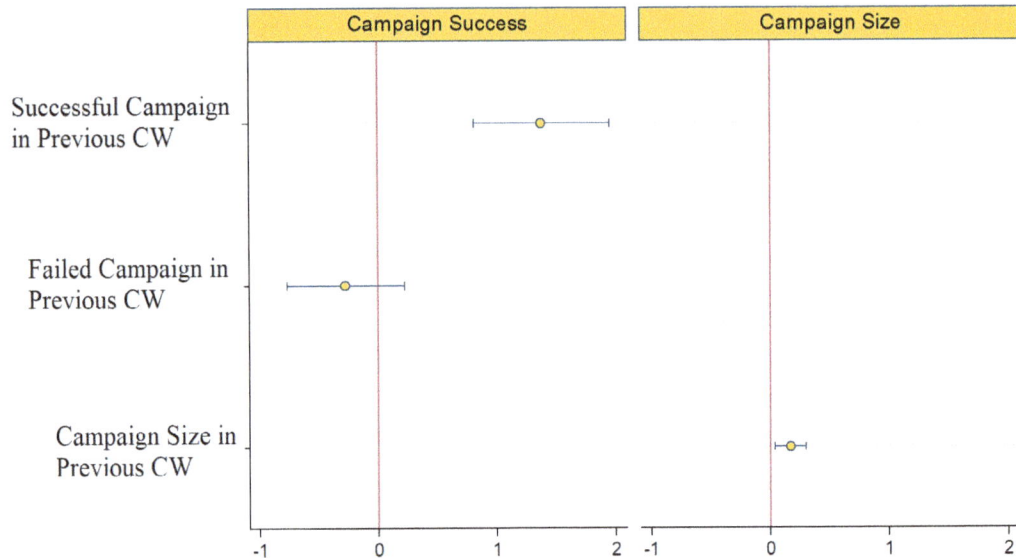

FIGURE 25. Logistic Regression Models: Nonviolent Campaign Success, Size, and Post–Conflict Democratic Transitions (1955–2010)

Post-conflict periods are more likely to witness post-conflict democratic transitions when wartime nonviolent campaigns exhibit greater social diversity, greater women's participation, and have more organizations within the movement. Nonviolent campaigns also appear to have a stronger legacy and impact on post-conflict democratization when they have decentralized campaign structures and have developed alternative institutions amid the context of civil war. This provides further evidence for Propositions 2c–8c.

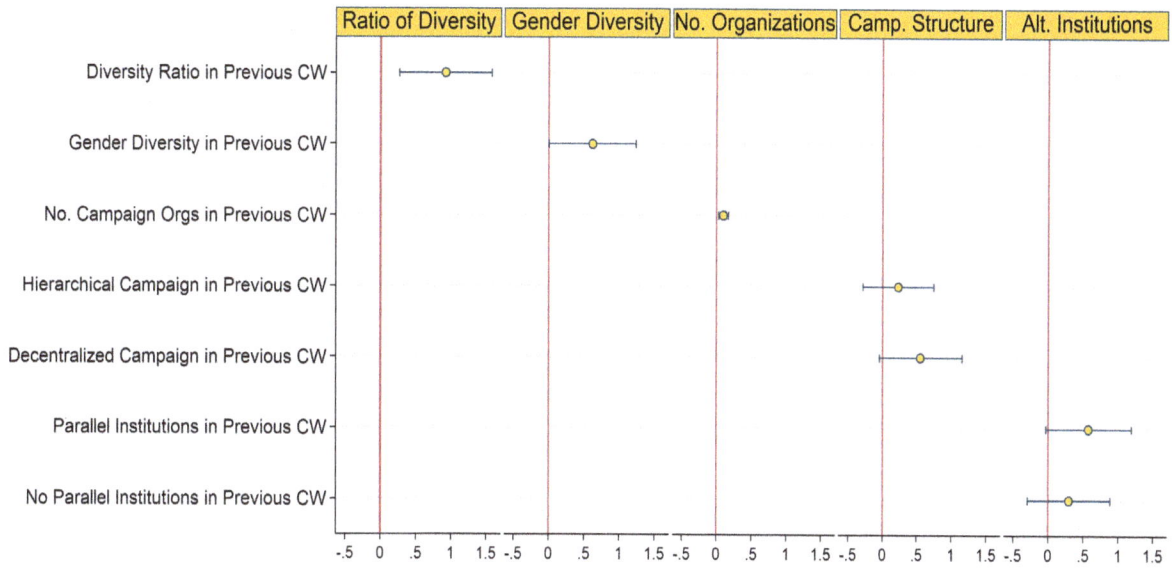

	Ratio of Diversity	Gender Diversity	No. Organizations	Camp. Structure	Alt. Institutions

Diversity Ratio in Previous CW

Gender Diversity in Previous CW

No. Campaign Orgs in Previous CW

Hierarchical Campaign in Previous CW

Decentralized Campaign in Previous CW

Parallel Institutions in Previous CW

No Parallel Institutions in Previous CW

-.5 0 .5 1 1.5 -.5 0 .5 1 1.5 -.5 0 .5 1 1.5 -.5 0 .5 1 1.5 -.5 0 .5 1 1.5

FIGURE 26. Logistic Regression Models: Other Nonviolent Campaign Attributes and Post-Conflict Democratic Transitions (1955–2010)

About the Author

Luke Abbs is a Fellow at the Centre of Religion, Reconciliation and Peace (CRRP), University of Winchester, and Associate Fellow at the Department of Government, University of Essex (since 2018). His research interests are nonviolent resistance and its impact on peace processes, religious peacebuilding, non-state armed actors, United Nations Peacekeeping, and mixed qualitative and quantitative methodology. Luke holds a PhD and MA in International Conflict Analysis from the University of Kent.